THE GLITTERING LAKE

Memoir of a District Officer in Kenya

BY

J.K.R. THORP

Copyright © 2012 J.K.R.Thorp

All rights reserved, including the right to reproduce this work, in whole or in part, in any form.

THE GLITTERING LAKE

FOR DOREEN AND ALISON

Figure 1: Lake Rudolf, an inhospitable shore

THE GLITTERING LAKE

"For a long time we gazed in speechless delight, spell-bound by the beauty of the scene before us, whilst our men, equally silent, stared into the distance for a few minutes, to break presently into shouts of astonishment at the sight of the glittering expanse of the great lake which melted on the horizon into the blue of the sky. At that moment, all our dangers, all our fatigues were forgotten in the joy of finding our exploring expedition crowned with success at last"

'Discovery by Count Teleki of Lakes Rudolph and Stefanie': by Ludwig Von Hohnel (Vol. II, p.95)

CONTENTS

Author's Note
Chapter 1   Lodwar
Chapter 2   Lokitaung
Chapter 3   Rumours of War
Chapter 4   Interlude
 Chapter 5   Marsabit
Chapter 6   War
Chapter 7   Aftermath
Chapter 8   Occasions and Reflections
Appendix   The Gelubba of the Omo Delta
Sketch Maps
1. Kenya
2. Western Lake Rudolph–Turkana District
3. The Lake Rudolph Region–Tribal Areas
4. Eastern Lake Rudolph- Marsabit District
Notes

All international boundaries are approximately as they were shown on maps in official use up to 1943 and they may not bear any relation to the actual boundaries today. Although Lake Rudolph is now officially known as Lake Turkana, the former name has been retained for the purpose of this book.

All illustrations are by the author.

AUTHOR'S NOTE

This book concerns an era of East African administration which has ended; that one which followed what can be termed the purely "law and order" era. It is about the day-to-day life of an ordinary Kenya District Officer during the period between the conquest of Ethiopia by Mussolini (1936) and the restoration of the Emperor Haile Selassie to the Imperial Throne (1941). It does not purport to set out, let alone offer, solutions for any of the tangled problems facing Kenya today, although it does, perhaps, indirectly illuminate more than one of those which are less well-known. In 1937, economics and social welfare had only just begun to be the concern of the field administration and even politics were no longer entirely unknown. Nevertheless, the time was still some way ahead when it was obligatory for a District Officer that he should solve all sorts of undefined and intangible conundrums. He was expected to do what was a more-or-less known job, or one the limits of which were at least roughly ascertainable. The intrinsic value of this job was not in dispute in any quarter. His human relations were so straightforward, happy and unpretentious that the phase was unknown; and his work was an end-in-itself. He was not yet expected to join the cast in a monster dramatic production on the international stage.

Although the Northern Province of Kenya covers 118,200 square miles (more than half of Kenya's total area of 225,000 square miles), it is the home of only about one hundred and seventy thousand people – a mere fraction of Kenya's population which at that time was over six million. The vast majority of the Province's inhabitants are nomads and they have few interests in common with the rest of their fellow country-men except, possibly, with the Masai at the opposite end of the territory; and they have but small knowledge of the Kenya which has taken so prominent a place in the British and American press during the last decades. Like two families living in a pair of semi-detached suburban villas, each half of Kenya has gone its own way, not liking very much what little it has picked up from time-to-time about the neighbour's way of life.

The Northern Province itself also falls neatly into two parts, on a line which can be very roughly drawn due south from the frontier station of Moyale. To the east of this line, the people are mostly Moslems and mostly Somalis; to the west, they are mostly pagans and only a very small number of Somalis live there. Owing to its racial, religious and cultural affinities with those territories to the east and north-east of Kenya, the eastern part of the Province has in more recent times generated some international interest. The western part, the Lake Rudolph region – for it is dominated by this great lake – has been of small interest to anyone but its inhabitants and to those who have in some way been professionally concerned with it. However, with tourist flights (shades of Count Teleki!) now operating to southern Lake Rudolph, it can no longer be said to be the *terra incognita* it was – or very certainly was until it became an operational area early in the Second World War. It is the Lake Rudolph region with which this book is primarily concerned.

Until sometime after the Second World War, what is now the Northern Province was administered as two separate areas; the Turkana Extra-Provincial District to the west of the Lake and the northern Frontier Extra-Provincial District to the east of the Lake, each being the administrative responsibility of an Officer-in-Charge, with headquarters at Kapenguria and Isiolo, respectively. They were, and no doubt still are, closed areas, to enter which non-residents required a permit under the Outlying Districts Ordinance to which a variety of conditions were attached, to suit the circumstances. In the case of persons travelling under their own steam, these conditions were mostly concerned with the permit-holder's personal safety, for travel was precarious and local resources insufficient to cope with more than an occasional search and rescue operation.

When I was undertaking the Colonial Service course at Cambridge University in 1934-35, prior to appointment as a District Officer (cadet) in Kenya, one of the various people who were kind enough to spend an evening talking to me and the other trainee cadets at the Colonial Service Club was Dr V.E. (now Sir Vivian) Fuchs. He had just returned from his Lake Rudolph-Rift Valley Expedition and he produced a mass of photographs for us to look at. There must have been something about his account of this remote area which especially fascinated me, because the images of several of his pictures were still clearly etched on my mind when it came to writing this book. At the time, the degree of reality in time and space which I attached to their subject-matter was approximately equivalent to that normally attached to the moon. I did not know then that four and a half out of the next eight years of my life would be spent in the region; and that the great Teleki's glittering lake (which he had discovered only forty-six years previously) with its sun-baked, empty approaches, space-fiction scenery and iron-tough nomadic peoples would become as familiar as anywhere I had known – or at any rate, as familiar as travelling some 3000 miles on foot or by camel and some 30,000 miles by truck (plus a modest 500 miles by air) can make anyone with 49,000 square miles of one of Africa's many empty spaces.

Lake Rudolph is about 180 miles long with a maximum width of 35 miles and is 1230 ft above sea level; Lake Victoria, by comparison, is some 3000 ft above sea level. Only one permanent river flows into it, the Omo, at the extreme northern tip, entering the Lake in a 20-mile wide delta that is almost impenetrable. The source of the Omo is seven hundred miles away in the Ethiopian highlands. The Lake has no outlet and contains three islands, the largest of which is South Island, a strange, volcanic, brooding, uninhabited place. Dr E.R. Worthington's Cambridge Expedition in 1930-31 established a depth of 240 feet in the neighbourhood of Central Island. This expedition was mainly concerned with the biology of the Lake while the main objectives of the Lake Rudolph- Rift Valley Expedition, in 1934, were geological and topographical survey work; other lines of scientific investigations were undertaken as well. Fuchs considered that between 1931 and 1934 the levels of the Lake had fallen by four feet and found that at its north-western corner the water did not exceed eight feet in depth for approximately two miles from the shore. He also estimated that during the forty-six years since the Lake's discovery, its level had dropped by at least 30 to 40 feet; and he was of the opinion that should the level continue to fall at the average speed maintained during the thirty years immediately preceding 1934, the northern shore of the Lake would have retreated by 1944 some ten miles from the then *de facto* boundary between Kenya and Ethiopia[1]. Fortunately, up to 1943 the behaviour of the Lake had continued to maintain a reputation for general unpredictability.

At the southern end of the Lake lies the Segupta Valley (sometimes known as the Segota Valley), some four hundred feet below the level of the lake. The average day-time temperature here is about 40^0 C. Within the Segupta Valley lie two small soda lakes, the Logipi and Alablab, home to thousands of flamingo. At the north end of the Valley is the Teleki Volcano, which erupted seven years after the Count had observed it. Together with Lake Rudolph, this Valley used to be part of one huge lake which extended a further one hundred miles south. Some fifteen thousand years ago, this enormous lake flowed into the Nile system through what is now the Lokitaung Gorge, crossing the Lotikipi Plains on the north-west side of Lake Rudolph. Petrified forest remains can still be found there. This northwest shore is also marked by the Murua Rithi Hills and the Lapur Mountain Range.

In writing this book, I wish to make the following acknowledgements: to my wife Doreen for much help and patience; to the Editor of the Kenya Weekly News for permission to reproduce parts of Chapter 3 and of the Appendix; to the Provincial Commissioner, Northern Province, for the official record of Mr Kier's death; to Sir Vivian Fuchs and to Mr H.P. Hall, of the Colonial Office, for lending me copies of various Lake Rudolph-Rift Valley Expedition publications – which are hard to come by in the Indian Ocean.

The official records of the Marsabit District seem to be just as palatable to termites today as they were twenty years ago - but I am grateful to the District Commissioner for having tried to find what I sought.

Although before the Second World War, it was usual to speak of "Abyssinia" and "Abyssinians", I have referred to "Ethiopia" and "Ethiopians" throughout, for sake of simplicity.

J.K.R.T.
Seychelles, 1961

Figure 2: A Turkana Elder

CHAPTER ONE

LODWAR

(1)

The western shore of Lake Rudolph is the eastern boundary of the Turkana District of Kenya. Lodwar, its 'capital', about 30 miles from the Lake and lies on a bend of the Turkwell River, a seasonal tributary. In 1937, Lodwar could produce little to justify the enormous letters in which the name was printed on most maps. The Turkwell River, like all the other rivers in the region, with the single exception of the Omo, had always felt that a few days flow each year was quite sufficient to ensure retention of its designation - on the same principle as the annual closure of a private road.

To meet the security requirements of an earlier (but not much earlier) times, the Lodwar administrative station had been sited on a small area of higher ground some 300 feet above lake level. It was within easy reach of the dry, sand-bed river from which water was available all the year round by digging. Apart from this, the site had nothing to commend it, for this strategically convenient promontory was a bare outcrop of almost red-hot, shiny lava rock. When in addition, the warm, dust-laden afternoon breeze rolled in uninhibited across the plains, you could be forgiven for thinking that some careless person had forgotten to shut the oven door. My first reaction on easing myself out of the well-worn military half-tonner which had brought me to this new home – battered, bemused, begrimed and extremely thirsty – was to wonder what strange devil must have been in possession when there had been born in me the ambition to become a member of His Majesty's Colonial Administrative Service.

The most prominent feature of the station was the small, triangular, loose-stone fort which was now used to house the police guardroom and the wireless station. Nearby, a new brick building of some magnificence contained the District Offices - except mine I soon discovered; the junior District Officer being still consigned to the outer and literal darkness of a small, mud rondavel. The complete absence of doors in the long building proclaimed to the newcomer that his work lay amongst honest, if not in other ways, an entirely law-abiding community. Behind it, there was a small, brick store in which high-octane petrol was kept for emergency use by the Royal Air Force. Between these two buildings, an enterprising District Commissioner had inserted an excellent squash court which had thus necessitated only a bare minimum of financial wangling. Opposite the District Offices and joining the two other sides of a rough square, were sundry mud-walled stores and the small brick medical dispensary which, boasting three or four beds, was called the Lodwar Hospital. Beyond these were the neat Kenya Police and Tribal Police lines and the quarters of the more menial grades of station staff.

The town consisted of half-a-dozen very dilapidated shacks, mostly owned by alien Somalis (that is to say, Somalis whose domicile was in British or Italian Somaliland and not in Kenya) and the residential area, sited at the river end of the lava plateau. This consisted of the houses of the District Commissioner, two District Officers, the Medical Officer and the three senior clerks.

New officers' and clerks' quarters of brick or undressed stone and built to a Sudan pattern, were being constructed but there were not yet enough to go around. As the latest arrival and most junior member of the administrative staff, I was conducted to the most palatial of the earlier type of residence. This was a mud-walled building comprising one large room which had been partitioned off to provide a store and a "bathroom" -

and having just open spaces to serve as doors and windows. It had a very low-pitched roof of brushwood - of Ethiopian style I was informed. This roof was certainly a good heat excluder; but I understood that if we should later receive our annual average of 1.5 inches of rain, it would become very clear that it could exclude little else. As no rain at all fell during my time in Lodwar, I never saw it put to the test.

Sweating porters unceremoniously dumped my kit in one corner of the house. I sat down on the nearest box, there being no furniture. I was not ruminating on what the Lake Rudolph area might hold for me during the next few years, nor even turning over in my mind what would be the most useful contribution I could make towards the welfare and progress of the Turkana. I was wondering what I did next, and why it should be necessary to do anything at all in such a stinking-hot, dusty, God-forsaken spot.

(2)

A few months later, having meanwhile imported some appropriately high-class furniture (fourth-hand), I moved into one of the new houses: two fair-sized rooms and a real bathroom below, with a screen sleeping-box on the flat roof. The interior was tastefully decorated in pale green. This was one of the four or five natural colours which we dug out of various volcanic deposits scattered around the district and from which we made all our own distempers. We lived on our roofs from 6 p.m. to 6 am and they were a real joy. My roof looked straight out over the vivid, green strip of the Turkwell River to the distant Uganda escarpment in the west and into the full glory of the wonderful sunsets. To the north, the little fort with its lone sentry on the walls and backed by the towering black cone of Lodwar Hill, both sharply etched against the rust-red evening sky, made as attractive an outpost of empire picture as one could wish And, although I do not recall that we ever felt frightfully imperial, we did feel and were, very outpost.

To the east of my rooftop, the lava plateau dropped sharply

away to a plain of firm sand known and sometimes used, as the aerodrome. At the river end of this plain, amongst the tall Dom palms, was what was known locally as the Royal Rudolph Golf Course. I should mention here that, at the Lodwar-Lokitaung crossroad, there was also the Royal Rudolph Hotel, a wall-less, thatched shack. A few years previously, an officer of the King's African Rifles got himself into considerable trouble by inserting advertisements in the East African Press that gave glowing accounts of the amenities provided by both these institutions. We seldom had any golf balls but the palm nuts – whose hard kernels were a source of vegetable ivory – made a sporting substitute. In this area there was also the graveyard. One of the three European graves was fairly new - that of a District Officer who had contracted a fatal illness during an unsuccessful search for two members of the Lake Rudolph-Rift Valley Expedition. These two men had visited South Island in Lake Rudolph and were never seen again. To this day, their fate remains one of those unsolved African mysteries.

Now it seemed to be the custom in most districts that a newly appointed officer should be at once taken to see the graveyard, where he could ponder on the various diseases which had accounted for some of his predecessors and on his own chance of survival. So indeed, two days after I had arrived in Kenya in 1935, with all the dire warnings of our Cambridge lecturer in Tropical Hygiene still buzzing unhappily through my mind, I found myself with my first District Commissioner in the graveyard at Kitui, some eighty miles east of Nairobi. I was struggling to remember how you avoided contracting blackwater fever. The Commissioner turned to me and looked me straight in the eyes.

"Do you know why I selected you out of the list of new cadets?" he suddenly asked.

"No, indeed, Sir," I respectfully replied.

"Well," he continued, "the Scottish poet Rabbie Burns once challenged a friend to produce the shortest possible epitaph for one Johnny Thorpe. 'That's easy,' said his friend, 'here lies the corp of Johnny Thorpe.' 'I can do better than that,' remarked Rabbie Burns, 'Thorpe's corpse.'" I gave a polite laugh but with little real feeling to it. "Yes," ruminated the District Commissioner with a smile, "I have always been greatly tickled by that epitaph. When I saw your name on the list it really did seem like a heaven-sent opportunity of possibly being able to make actual use of it myself!"

Our water supply system, both hot and cold, was simple. In the morning, a string of camels carted water in twelve-gallon copper containers (called barramils) from a central tank, into which water was pumped from shallow wells in the sandy riverbed. The barramils were dumped on the ground outside the houses, some being immediately carried up the outside steps on to the roof where the water was tipped into a storage tank. This was the cold supply. By evening, the water in those barramils left lying outside was very much too hot for a hot bath.

There was no soil at Lodwar and such fresh vegetables as we got came up once a week from the highland station of Kapenguria (our administrative headquarters), almost two hundred miles south close to the border with Uganda. George Chaundy, the Principal of the Kapenguria Government African School, was by profession an agricultural officer. He made a special thing of supplying us with vegetables and we blessed him for it. During his time, the supply never failed, although delays *en route* frequently meant that many of his beautiful and treasured vegetables were quite limp by the time we received them. We did manage to grow excellent mint in our bathwater drains. Seeing that our staple diet was mutton and goat, a beneficent Providence must have had some hand in this.

By complicated manipulation of my own bathwater drain, I once succeeded in growing a masterly crop of tomatoes along one side of my house. It was a minor sort of Jack and the Beanstalk and the tendrils spread out so strongly and so quickly that I was hard put expanding the rough trellis work rapidly enough to keep up with them. My success was, I feel sure, entirely due to the regular application of a lurid, green, iron tonic which the

Medical Officer acquired in comparatively large quantities as free samples. Until recent times, Northern and Southern Turkana had been separate districts, with a total of five stations and sub-stations: Lodwar, Kaputir, Kolossia, Kakuma and Lokitaung, of which only Lodwar and Lokitaung now remained. (The sub-stations of Kolossia and Kakuma could, between them, probably have claimed the all-African record for sending officers 'round the bend'). The purveyors of patent medicines and other medical supplies had not yet caught up with these changes and samples arrived addressed separately and in great profusion to the Medical Officer, Northern Turkana, Southern Turkana, Lodwar, Kaputir, Kolossia, Kakuma and Lokitaung.

About a week after I arrived in Lodwar, there had been great excitement in the Turkana medical world: for the first time on record, a Turkana woman had been successfully cajoled into having her baby in the small hospital. She was duly admitted, pampered and admired and all seemed to be going splendidly – including the Medical Officer's article for 'The Lancet'. As her time approached, this poor paragon of progress became more and more agitated. When things started happening, she completely lost her nerve and bolted for the aerodrome. Her fine baby was duly born in comfort and in the traditional manner behind a bush. It was a long time before a woman of stern, pioneering spirit was to come forward and stay the full course.

The Medical Officer, like the rest of us, spent a great deal of time on safari. It was regarded as inevitable that something outlandish would happen immediately he left the station. My own first such crisis was when one of the Goan clerks threw a most violent epileptic fit in the office. On another occasion, the Medical Officer had hardly receded from sight when the African dresser rushed into my office in a great panic to say that a police corporal's wife was vomiting a snake. I did not have time to look up the implications of such a remarkable symptom in the fat wad of First Aid notes I had so carefully recorded at Cambridge before he ushered in the woman. Between us, we helped the unfortunate woman to relieve herself of several yards of tapeworm. This we carefully and neatly wound on to my round office ruler and then equally carefully unwound into my tin wash basin. I was assured later, by the highest authority, that the ejection of a tapeworm orally was a most unusual occurrence, a statement for which I was

Figure 3: (top) Lodwar, the author's first home, (bottom) Lodwar, the residential area with a modern house in the background

Figure 4: (top) Lodwar, the station water supply in action, (bottom) Lodwar, R.A.F. Vickers Vincents on the aerodrome

THE GLITTERING LAKE

Figure 5: (top) Sgt. Farah Issa, the Kenya Police, (bottom) Lodwar Fort and changing of the guard

Figure 6: (top) Sgt. Amajong, Turkana Tribal Police, (bottom) Turkana Tribal Police guard of honour for His Excellency the Governor

most profoundly thankful. On other occasions, it was the dresser who was absent - and I would be called in by the Medical Officer to administer an anaesthetic. It was a simple enough matter to shake ether on to the mask and with a dry "theatre" temperature of about 110^0 F, not a very dangerous one. The trick to be mastered was to keep myself from going under before the patient or – even more important – from going under while the operation was in progress.

Contrary to general opinion, life in places like Lodwar is a problem only for those completely unsuited to them by temperament. Some people, indeed, are so unsuited - and it was with relief I soon discovered that I was not one of them. Office hours were from 7.30 a.m. to 2 p.m., with a station inspection at 6 a.m. It was unusual for more than one of the three administrative officers to be in the station at the same time and as a result, there was always more than enough work to be done. In addition to correspondence, report writing and accounting, hearing civil and criminal cases, settling complaints and interviewing all and sundry, there was always building and other work in the station to be planned and executed; and (there being no Police Officer) the units of forty Kenya Police and thirty Tribal Police to be drilled and trained. In addition, for juniors like me, compulsory language and law examinations loomed darkly ahead. After lunch, we sweated it out indoors. During my Lodwar afternoons, I unsuccessfully completed a correspondence course in short-story writing (they make it sound so easy) and completely failed to master the Hawaiian guitar – although I reached the stage of being able to render "Turkey in the Straw" to derisive applause. The sun was still scorching hot at 5 p.m. but a walk, a game of squash, partridge shooting along the banks of the Turkwell or a place in a scratch football team gave one enough exercise – and also a two-guinea thirst which, contrary to common opinion, was not quenched solely with alcohol.

Small, isolated communities, such as ours at Lodwar, become very self-contained and self-sufficient. Loneliness either drives you crazy - or its attractions quickly grow on you. In the first case, it is as well to get out as smartly as you can; in the second, to make up your mind firmly, from the beginning, that it is only an episode in your life, of limited duration – otherwise you may find yourself permanently estranged from any more civilised kind of existence.

Apart from the occasional visiting official, we seldom saw anyone from the outside world. Even these were rare birds, for we had no truck with the heads of Departments; and "experts" were less common then than now. We had a visit from one grassland expert who subsequently advised that if we wanted to establish reasonable grazing in the district, we would, first, have to kill the termites by applying a generous sprinkling of camphor to the whole countryside. A very occasional hunting or fishing safari came through on the way to the Lake. They always tried to be friendly and sympathetic. They assumed that their mere presence must be bringing great joy into our boring and lonely lives; but we found *them* boring and were always glad to see them leave – when it had proved impractical to avoid meeting them in the first place. Our aloofness and lack of enthusiasm for their company surprised and rather hurt them. It all seems a little silly looking back on it now - but we managed somehow to work up quite a hate for them.

(3)

The nearest point on Lake Rudolph, by road, was Ferguson Gulf, about halfway up the west side of the Lake. Visits here were ninety per cent fun and ten per cent work. It was only in later years that I came to connect visits to the Lake with anything other than straight recreation. It was in a state of some excitement that I set off on my first visit to Ferguson Gulf. However, by the time the truck had been coaxed to the end of the track which petered out in dry, pot-holed mud flats, my enthusiasm had dwindled to nil. There was nothing visible but apparently endless, tall reed banks. We eventually came to some water and, piling into two Government-owned, flat-bottomed, high-powered boats, we pushed off down the channel between this towering reed vegetation. The type of boat was the Norwegian Pram which seemed a most inappropriate boat in that hot climate. We eventually reached more open water. As we splashed along, vast clouds of water birds rose into the air until the sky around us was a dark, whirling mass of cormorants, herons, ibis and duck – Pintail, Gargeny, Teal and Shoveller – with Egyptian Geese flapping desperately to gain height whilst flotillas of pelicans behaved for all the world like overloaded flying boats straining to become airborne. At certain times of the year, the commonest duck, what we called the Whistling Teal, could possibly be counted in millions. The more correct name for this duck was the Whistling Tree Duck. The inner part of the Gulf was only a couple of feet deep but we were soon out into deeper water and moving towards a sand-spit which jutted out at the further side of its mouth. On this sand-spit were several palm-thatched shelters which were used as a rest house.

Under a scheme started some years previously, a splendid character called Pangrassio had been brought from Lake Victoria to Ferguson Gulf to teach the Turkana how to use boats and to fish with seine nets, a job he had already most successfully accomplished. I met him for the first time on this trip to the sand-spit and by way of opening the conversation I said: "Are there any fish in the Lake, Pangrassio?" To this rather naïve question he replied scathingly: "Yes, sir, its half fish and half water!" And this statement was not far from the truth for the Lake teemed with fish. I had hardly been on the sand-spit for ten minutes when Pangrassio and his team swiftly laid their net with the boat, hauled the net ashore and cast at my feet more than twenty large Tilapia, a very good fish to eat. Nile Perch up to fifty pounds or more were common. The record up to that time, I believe, was three hundred and fifty pounds. Tiger fish and other spiny types abounded in the shallows.

During my time in Lodwar, I tried out a whole range of patent lures and baits to catch the all-time monster perch. Some of these lures were so beautifully coloured and did such amazing things in the water that it was hard to believe that any fish could possibly ignore them – indeed I felt sometimes like eating them myself they looked so alluring. I never caught any perch that way, nor did I succeed in shooting them lying basking in the sun on the lake surface, although in desperation I tried that, too. It was only on my very last day that I had any success: I caught three large perch with lumps of tiger fish casually stuck on the end of an ordinary meat hook.

One of the effects of having so much fish in the lake (only the lowest caste of Turkana would eat them – but they ate anything, including slightly decomposed crocodile) was that the ordinary run of really enormous lake crocodiles was so well fed that it did not worry about either human beings or goats. The crocodiles living at the very north end of the lake, where the Omo River poured in fresh water from the Ethiopian Highlands, behaved quite differently and relished the occasional juicy steak from the shore.

The odd days and weekends we were able to spend at Ferguson Gulf – swimming, fishing, boating, shooting and idling – were a joy and made up for the intervening months of dirt, dust, footslogging and the eternal, all-pervading smell of goat and sheep.

THE GLITTERING LAKE

Figure 7: Ferguson Gulf: the author's only catch of Nile Perch

Figure 8: (top) FergusonGulf: Hauling in a Seine net, (bottom) Ferguson Gulf: Harpoonists on the shore of Lake Rudolf

Figure 9: (top) Medical Officer's clinic near Ferguson Gulf, (bottom) Prospective patients.

Figure 10: Ferguson Gulf: Turkana fishermen.

Figure 11: Watering cattle from a well.

THE GLITTERING LAKE

Figure 12: (top) Kakuma: the abandoned sub-station, (bottom) Greeting the District Officer.

Figure 13: (top) Impromptu dance at 6.30 a.m., (bottom) Ceremonial headdress

THE GLITTERING LAKE

(4)

The Turkana tribe drew an unlucky number in the Pax Britannica lottery of the late 19th and early 20th Century. Having, by misfortune as it were, established themselves in the arid, desert country which lies between Lake Rudolf and the lengthy, clear-cut escarpment which is now the Kenya-Uganda boundary, there they had to stay put. Left to themselves, they would possibly by now be living in the fertile highland country to the south-west and south and perhaps even further afield. The land which they presently occupy would have been filled up by some other tribes now living in the Sudan or south-west Ethiopia; for a general north-south population movement and pressure stretches back beyond the dawn of African History. That their progress in a more-or-less southerly direction was so barred was a stroke of luck for various other tribes; for the Turkana were a strong and virile people, great fighting men and well organised for war. They did not accept their lottery ticket without protest; and for the best of part of two decades they did their best to improve their position to the west and south-west at the expense of their Karamajong and Suk neighbours. The Turkana, in fact, made their protests so vigorously and caused so much bloodshed and disturbance that, during the period of the First World War, a major, punitive expedition was launched against them with units of the King's African Rifles and Masai levies, in an attempt to establish permanent peace in the area. While the Turkana did not take all this lying down, they were inevitably defeated and suffered heavy losses in both manpower and stock. Quite unnecessarily heavy, we thought, but it is easy to condemn the actions of one's predecessors out of context; and to judge them by standards of public conscience which were then unknown. The tribe gradually recovered some of its strength, although many families and individuals were permanently impoverished. It was typical of the Turkana's attitude to life that they bore no permanent grudge against authority. They were warriors and it was accepted that they had been defeated in war.

Only a bare twenty years later, the Turkana were on the best of terms with the King's African Rifles, whose role now was to protect them from the north. I thought it more than a nominal privilege to serve with such a friendly and loyal people. Their friendship and loyalty were frequently demonstrated in concrete fashion and for which it would have been difficult to trace any mercenary or other ulterior motive; for they received little from us except for this protection which was far from being perfect. Every few years, our defences would prove inadequate and the northern sections of the tribe would be swiped by raiders from across the border. As one of my predecessors in Lodwar put, in a safari report: 'It was difficult sometimes to see what great advantage accrued to the Turkana from belonging to the British Empire, except for an infinitesimal share in ruling the waves.'

However, one thing could be said. As a result of all the earlier unpleasantness, fighting and punitive looting, at least the majority of the fifty-three thousand or so members of the tribe could now lead their lives in peace; their recognised rights to water and grazing were upheld; and a start was being made in providing medical services and other amenities in this most inhospitable land. It has, of course, long since become the fashion to forget what an astonishing and miraculous event was the mere establishment of internal peace and a fair degree of orderly existence in such places as these remote northern wastes of Kenya, notwithstanding the fact that it all took place comparatively recently. To these nomads, that otherwise ubiquitous pointer to progress, the pit latrine, was a non-starter - but such peace as we could give them was something they had come to value greatly.

(5)

I had already spent two years in the Kamba districts of Kitui and Machakos, some forty miles south-east of Nairobi, before I went to Turkana; but I was still quite unprepared for the wild and desolate environment of the Lake Rudolph region. It is from these parts, especially from the southern Lake area, that the personnel for the first moon landing-party should be recruited. The temperature might be a snag but otherwise they would feel quite at home.

Living in a male nudist colony took a little getting used for, in the traditional Nilo-Hamitic fashion, the Turkana men went about their day stark naked. It was a form of dress admirably suited to the climate. Within a couple of weeks, I saw nothing at all incongruous in having a group of naked men standing in front of me in the office, arguing vociferously about who owed to whom how many goats. On formal occasions, it was customary to wear a short elbow-length skin cape; or if you were an elder, then also on certain informal occasions. Otherwise, all sartorial effort was put into headdress and facial, leg and arm ornaments. The basis of the headdress was a carefully made and shaped mudpack, with small, permanent holes into which feathers could be inserted according to taste. For everyday wear, two or three ostrich feathers were adequate but on special occasions the Turkana really let themselves go.

While I was stationed at Lodwar, we were paid a visit by the Governor of Kenya, the late Sir Robert Brooke-Popham, only the second gubernatorial visit to have been made since the Turkana had first been under British administration. Literally weeks were spent by hundreds of men in preparing the most elaborate and colourful headdresses, some of the wearers of which made journeys of up to twelve days in order to attend His Excellency's *baraza* with tribal representatives. The Governor, as an Air Chief Marshall, was the possessor of one of the most glamorous of all service dress uniforms but, for this occasion, he wore only a khaki shirt and shorts and a rather worn khaki helmet with an RAF flash. The Turkana themselves probably never gave the matter a thought - but we regarded it as an unspeakable let-down by someone.

Denis McKay was District Commissioner for the duration

of my stay in Turkana. He was an understanding type and the restoration of my morale - which had started during the few months in my previous district - continued. Before that, I had been some eighteen months – my first in Kenya – under a DC whom I later (much later) came to admire but whose cadet-baiting was notorious. His many excellent qualities were more apparent to me and my contemporaries at a distance, in both time and place. It was not so much that I objected to his not suffering fools gladly (and I felt a complete idiot after my first ten minutes with him) but I thought his attitude of 'I'll teach this young pup that he does not know everything' grossly unfair - for I was already correctly convinced that I knew nothing. If this ignorance shone too clearly through my conversation, there was nothing to be done about it – for to have remained completely silent would probably have created an even worse impression.

Denis McKay ran his district with a minimum of red tape and an abhorrence of "bull". We rather prided ourselves on our easy-going informality, which we felt to be in striking contrast to what we understood happened on the other side of the Lake. Not, indeed, that we knew very much about what happened over there, for in those days we were very parochial in our outlook and knowledge; communications across the Lake were almost nil. However, the wording of the occasional wireless message which we did receive seemed to indicate that a different system was in operation and we fairly snorted with disdain. I think the senders must sometimes have been very puzzled at the terms in which our replies were couched. Later, I gained an intimate knowledge of the 'rod of iron' system which had become traditional in the Northern Frontier District. The results did not seem much different from ours in Turkana – and I'm sure we were a lot happier.

The establishment of administrative officers was four: one District Commissioner and two District Officers at Lodwar; and a District Officer in charge of the Lokitaung sub-station in the north. I was assigned the area north and north-east of Lodwar and John Dowson dealt with the area south of Lodwar. The main purposes when touring our areas were the collection of poll-tax (payable by all male adult Turkana), ensuring the proper enforcement of livestock grazing and watering (including issuing the various orders which were necessary to operate the system in accordance with rainfall and state of the grazing lands), settling internal disputes and various individual quarrels and maintaining inter-tribal peace along our borders. Touring was essential work and, so long as the officers were constantly out in the district, few problems of any serious nature arose. When the Turkana failed to see an officer for any length of time, they tended to forget they were being administered and there was apt to be trouble.

The poll tax did not seem excessive at 3/- or one sheep or goat per annum but many could not afford it and were exempted *ad hoc* from payment. It was the principle of no administration without taxation which was deemed important. Money, of course, was a meaningless commodity to the Turkana and most of the tax was collected in kind.

Payment in kind was accounted through a system called the Turkana Suspense Account. I never really understood how this device worked and, judging from the correspondence and sheaves of audit queries it caused, I doubt if anyone did from the Accountant –General and the Director of Audit downwards. To make the accounting less involved than it would otherwise have been, we carried with us on safari a few hundred silver shillings – notes being totally unacceptable to the Turkana. With this liquid reserve, we bought the sheep and goats at 3/- each and then solemnly collected the 3/- back in payment of tax for which a receipt was issued. However, there was very much more to it than that.

The sheep and goats we bought were issued as rations to the Police and King's African Rifles and to other Government staff. It sounds simple enough to buy one goat for 3/-, to credit the owner with 3/- payment of his tax and to issue the goat, at the same value, as someone else's rations for a certain length of time (all sheep and goats were deemed to produce 20 lb of meat). However, it never seemed to work out quite like that. Goats became sick, or ran away or died; or were eaten as rations before they ever got near Lodwar – and all this was going on simultaneously all over the district. The main Suspense Account herd was kept at Lodwar. However, most of the time there were sub-herds on their way to the KAR at Lokitaung, as well as small safari and Police post ration groups scattered over some 23,000 square miles of Africa. It drove the Treasury boys in Nairobi crazy and they, in turn, took it out on us.

Tax collection has a prosaic sound to it and conjures up visions of bespectacled clerks behind counters, either looking very disdainfully at the taxpayer or, with their heads buried in the records, very obviously ignoring him. But there was nothing prosaic about tax collection in Turkana, it being a question of 'first catch your goat'. It was indeed a most colourful and athletic undertaking, the funny side of which took the sting out of it for even the most reluctant taxpayer.

Shortly after my arrival in Lodwar, I was sent to the Oripoi valley in the north-west, to inspect and re-provision the police post there, to settle some outstanding disputes and to collect tax on the way. It was my first taste of safari in the region and it followed a pattern which was to become very familiar. However, during this first tour, I made two mistakes which I never made again. The first mistake was that I very nearly allowed myself to be caught camping in a dry, sand river (the shady trees being irresistible). Heavy rain falling hundreds of miles away in Uganda caused the sand river to flash flood with little warning and it was only by good luck that our party escaped without disastrous consequences. The second mistake was that I lost my baggage camels. Either mistake could have brought this story to a sad and untimely end.

The start of any camel safari was always chaotic but on this first occasion I felt it must be all entirely my own fault; I despaired of ever getting off at all. Ropes broke and two camel-leaders had a fight. An old soldier of a camel stoutly resisted all efforts to load him. A young camel bolted, boxes burst open and bags split. Eventually, we set off, enclosed in an invisible but quite tangible aura of bad temper on the part of both man and beast.

The size of a safari depended partly on how many people were going and how far and partly on the maximum distance between water holes *en route*. Rations for the whole party for the entire trip had to be taken - and also sufficient water to cover the waterless gaps. The load of water for a camel was 24 gallons. In addition to me, an average routine safari would consist of an interpreter, a cook, a personal servant, three Kenya police, four tribal police and up to half-a-dozen camel leaders. A Kenya Police sergeant or corporal would be in charge: responsible for discipline, organisation and technical competence of the party – all three desiderata being subject to variation.

It was a remarkable thing how after the most inauspicious of starts, the safari would settle down, even the camels becoming quite cheerful – if that adjective can ever be applied to a camel. As soon as we got a march away from the station, we were on our own, a self-contained unit entirely responsible for its own safety and welfare. Except on the very unusual occasion when rain was expected, we used no tents. We slept in the open at night and rested beneath the best shade we could find during the hottest hours of the day. Fresh meat rations were issued daily; and a carefully calculated number of sheep and goats set out with us from the station unless it was expected that tax goats would be collected within a day or so. Something I never quite got over during the next four and a half years was the pathetically dwindling safari herd. It seemed less pathetic when we collected a few thousand head *en route*. But that little herd of twenty or thirty which left the station so sleek and frisky, never to return, always struck me as a tragic band of animals, sacrificed to meet our unworthy cravings for fresh meat. Not indeed that I let such thoughts spoil my appetite, for nothing tasted better than a fresh mutton chop eaten in the open air after a twenty-five-mile walk; or liver and bacon at 10 a.m. when you had been walking since before dawn. I was only unfortunate that it was more frequently goat which appeared as the *plat du jour*.

Safari in Turkana conditions mostly consisted of walking a very long way to do what seemed very little and, sometimes, to do nothing at all. The people you expected to find at a certain place might have moved somewhere else by the time you had arrived there. Unless there was some reason for doing longer or shorter journeys, we aimed at about twenty miles each day. When the going was good, we did three miles an hour or about seven to eight hours of walking in all. It was usual to start the day at about 5.30 a.m. and stop at the best available shade (or what had to pass as shade) at about 9.30 a.m. We would stay there for breakfast and lunch, the camels being put out to browse whatever sparse bushes and trees were in the vicinity. We moved on at about 3 p.m. after the hottest part of the day had passed, finally halting for the night at about 6 or 6.30 p.m.

One of the most important duties of the NCO in charge of the safari was rationing food and water. He was responsible for the slaughter of the day's meat when we camped in the morning, for the issue of dry rations and, above all, for the issue of water rations morning and evening. Water discipline was essential when what you carried had to last for a fixed time. As an extra precaution against the over-thirsty, the water containers were usually stacked near my bed at night. One of the many useful things the desert taught me was to keep thirst under control. Quite early on, I trained myself never to drink on the march, however great the temptation in those blistering temperatures.

When the evening camp had been set up and that heavenly moment had arrived when the heat lost its kick as the sun at last slipped below the horizon, then the NCO in charge would march up to me, clean, sober and properly dressed, to make his daily report. Standing at the slope and slapping his rifle hard in a salute worthy of a well-trained parade ground sergeant, he would say "Report, sir!" Then would follow a list of everything we had: so many barramils full of water and so many empty; the number of camels and sacks of flour; the number of rifles and rounds of ammunition. Then followed details of our personnel: "Four Kenya Police (including myself), sir! Six tribal police, five camel leaders, one cook, one servant, one interpreter and one officer, sir!" It was always a relief to be able to relax over a drink in the sure knowledge that one was known to be present and, possibly, correct.

When one arrived near a Turkana encampment, the people turned up early. It was the custom for the men to approach our camp in a solid phalanx, in slow time and singing a deep-throated chant, accompanied by a rhythmical up-and-down movement of their spears. This approach ceremony might take anything up to half an hour and often concluded with a wild charge which would suddenly stop when only about two feet from where I would be sitting. At first, I found this very unnerving. The Turkana would then sit round in a half-circle, the elders in front. After an initial exchange of courtesies, I would hear their news, arrange to deal with any individual complaints and give such advice and instructions as seemed to be needed (and if I could think of any at all). After this, there was the tax to be collected and here the fun began.

As I mentioned before, tax was mostly paid in kind. First, I had to pass the individual sheep or goat as being of a suitable standard. I then purchased the sheep or goats for cash at 3/- each, passing them into the care of the Tribal Police, to become honoured members of the Suspense Account herd. Gratefully and with as much dignity as I could muster, I then accepted back the amount I had just paid out, in payment of poll tax. The same money was used over-and-over again, to the extent that the number of sheep and goats tendered made this necessary. In theory, the whole scheme was as simple and foolproof as the ABC - but desert-bred goats and fat-tailed sheep have minds of their own. They frequently objected more strongly than their owners to being handed over as tax. They would make quick dashes for safety and anyone not already preoccupied with his own animals would join in vigorous efforts to catch them. Goat-catching was, in fact, a very skilled job and one at which, from long practice, many of the Tribal Police excelled. In the annual sports at Lodwar, we usually included a goat-catching competition for the Tribal Police. These would be released in pairs to catch the wildest and wiliest members of the Suspense Account herd. The ingenuity displayed by both man and goat was remarkable and the event always generated great excitement and enthusiasm amongst the spectators.

The Turkana Tribal Police Unit was a very tough and a very smart body of men and they sometimes performed outstanding feats of endurance. In emergency, they could cover astounding distances at great speed; and they could always be trusted to carry out, to their best ability, whatever orders they were given. On one occasion, a Lodwar shop employee was wanted for the petty offence of stealing a pair of shorts. He was thought to be in hiding a few miles away. I instructed one of the less impressive-looking tribal police (most were well over six feet tall) to locate the offender and arrest him. I forgot all about the incident until about six weeks later the tribal policeman turned up at my office with the man, carrying the missing pair of shorts. It was only by chance that I asked the policeman where he had found the man. He told me that he had learned that the offender was not where we had assumed him to be but had surreptitiously left the Turkana district in a trader's truck for a town in another district. The tribal policeman had taken what he termed a 'shortcut' by walking 200 miles, had then contacted the local police, found the wanted man and walked him back the 200 miles to Lodwar. He did not even hint that he had done anything over and above his simple duty and, to give the offender some credit, he had no complaints either.

The Tribal Police uniform was a short, dark blue 'kilt' with a red border, white goatskin gaiters, red and white feathers in the mud-pack headdress, a cartridge belt and a rifle. On ceremonial occasions, when the policemen were really spruced up, they looked magnificent, as indeed they were. While I was stationed at Lodwar, the only full-scale ceremonial Guard of Honour we turned out was for the visit of the Governor of Kenya. He remarked afterwards that it was the most impressive guard ever mounted for him and I have no doubt that he meant it.

(6)

It is a fact – and a rather sad one – that one rapidly becomes accustomed to new surroundings - however strange they might be. After one or two months in Turkana, I could imagine no other landscape or alternative way of life. Kenya – on both sides of the Lake we always referred to 'Kenya' as if it were another country altogether – seemed as unreal to us as another planet. Our reality lay in the great, empty plains with the ever-present mirage shimmering in the near distance; in the giant anthills stretching in all directions like a vast, deserted factory town with its tall, grey chimney stacks; in the broad belts of vivid greenery, marking the dry river beds, winding snake-like across the plains until they were stopped by the shores of the great Lake; in the hazy, blue mountains which always seemed to be far away; and in the pitch-black, lava outcrops and the immense, tumbled, larval slag-heaps which lay scattered about like remnants of a dead and long-forgotten world.

Some months after my arrival, there were alarms and excursions on the Uganda border, when bands of armed Suk decided they would use Turkana grazing and watering points whether permitted or not. In the end, the activity amounted to little but some very bad feeling and a great deal of heated argument. This was extinguished only after we had inserted fair-sized parties of Police between the excited contestants. One result, however, was a decision that I should participate in a joint boundary touring safari with my opposite number in the Ugandan town of Moroto, Percy Minns. As this neighbouring Ugandan station (headquarters of the Karamoja District) was sited on the top of the escarpment - and in the shadow of the magnificent mountain from which it took its name - I was delighted at the chance of seeing and doing something different.

The District Commissioner, Karamoja, was a famous character known to all as Uncle Tom Preston. He had already been in Moroto for more than twenty years. In Turkana, we regarded him as a hopeless proposition when it came to any form of intertribal quarrel. He had become so devoted to his own 'parishioners' that he could see no wrong in anything they did; nor could he bear to do anything but back them to the hilt in all circumstances. Tom Preston seemed to have lost the capacity for objective judgement and was a good example of the disadvantages attached to the leaving of an administrative officer for too long in one district – for there were disadvantages, whatever the better-known arguments in favour of maintaining 'continuity'.

Figure 14: (top) Moroto: Uncle Tom Preston (in dressing gown) and Percy Minns,
(bottom) Capt. John Keane, 4th K.A.R., and a typical Turkana ant hill.

I arrived in Moroto late one afternoon. On seeing the smooth, green lawns, the shady trees, the beautiful roses in the garden, a lovely stream bubbling down the hillside and feeling a distinctly cold nip in the air, I knew I had reached heaven. I found it hard to believe that this was regarded as one of Uganda's more unpleasant and remote outposts. They even lived in houses that looked like houses, with masses of government supplied furniture.

Uncle Tom was neither fierce nor rude as I had been led to expect but in every other way he came up to expectations. His favourite drink was sherry and bitter and he took active steps to ensure that his guests kept pace with him. Being no great drinker myself, I somehow managed to get away with one drink to every three of his. I consumed the unprecedented total of seven plus a couple poured into a convenient flowerpot. We sat down to dinner just after midnight. A few years later, Uncle Tom finally retired and decided, I believe, to spend the remainder of his life in the Seychelle Islands. On his way down to the Kenya coast, he met an old friend from the King's African Rifles camped on the roadside not many miles from Moroto. Their first evening together was so congenial and convivial that the two friends stayed there on the roadside for another ten days. Tom Preston then moved down to Kitale where he spent a night in the Kitale Hotel, the bill for which was said to have amounted to a total of £50, a considerable sum in those days. I subsequently heard that he died in Mombasa while waiting for his ship to the Seychelles, a sad ending for a lonely man - but perhaps a colourful conclusion to a colourful life.

CHAPTER TWO

LOKITAUNG

(1)

When I took over the Lokitaung sub-station from Jack Wolff, the circumstances of the handover turned out to be a little unusual. Lokitaung was, and still is, considered to be one of the most remote locations in Kenya. Jack had just returned from local leave, complaining of an itching bite on his arm. This he presumed to be a final fling by the Nairobi mosquitoes which in those days were both widespread and of notorious voracity. Indeed, one of the places where they had achieved their greatest notoriety was the European Hospital, the current jest being that one went in with a broken leg and came out with cerebral malaria. Next morning, Jack had a moderate temperature and a swollen arm with a few nasty, red streaks spreading up it. I myself had a raging temperature and a fit of shakes caused by a serious bout of malaria.

Dr Jaswant Singh, the admirable Lokitaung sub-assistant surgeon, put us to bed side by side in the small, single room which comprised the District Officer's house. Prosepticine was then the new wonder drug, so a wireless message was sent to Nairobi for supplies of it to come up on that week's KAR convoy. In those days, it was unheard of to have any such medical luxury in a place like Lokitaung. Jaswant Singh's kindly, bearded face looked graver each day, although he did his best to keep us cheerful. Muzzy with quinine and feeling extremely weak, I used to watch him squeeze foul-looking puss out of Jack's arm as if from a giant tube of toothpaste, pretending I did not notice any difference in the length of the red streaks.

The wonder drug arrived just in time to save Jack. I felt he could hardly last much longer. I threw off my attack of malaria and we managed some very half-hearted handing and taking over ceremonies. Jack departed Lokitaung bequeathing me, besides the problems of his sub-district, a spare tube of Prosepticine tablets and two delightful but, unhappily, rickets-ridden cheetahs. I did my best for these cheetahs with every calcium product the hospital, the KAR stores and a Nairobi chemist could supply. I nearly broke my neck shooting birds for them to eat, unplucked: a feather diet, I was assured by experts, was highly anti-rickets. All this effort was to no avail and they had to be destroyed.

Lokitaung sub-station was in a pass in the Labur range of mountains, to the north-west of Lake Rudolph and, at some 2000 feet above sea-level, was noticeably cooler than Lodwar. The District Officer's house, (although it was more of a hut than a house), was located on the edge of a cliff that overlooked the deep and narrow Lokitaung Gorge. A rather sketchy and, in some places, hair-raising road curled down this gorge for seven miles, to debouch on the plain running down to the Lake shore. On one side of the single-roomed house (built of stone with a thatched roof) was an open mud-and-wattle rondavel which I soon found to be the best place for my bedroom. On the other side there was a small storeroom. The administrative staff consisted of myself, a delightful, pock-marked simian character called Longaria who was interpreter and general factotum, one Kenya Police corporal and two constables, six Tribal Police and twenty Turkana Frontier Scouts. My small flagpole planted in the ground outside my house had the distinction of being very crooked and joined in three places. This was because no single pole of more than four or five feet in length could be found anywhere in the neighbourhood. A strong, dusty wind blew in irregular gusts all day and most nights. After a while, it made one want to scream – but I soon found this behaviour had no effect on it whatsoever. It was the only intolerable feature of the place.

Lokitaung was essentially a military post and was garrisoned by a company of the 4th (Uganda) King's African Rifles, with a signallers and a heavy machine-gun section. The machine-gunners and signallers lived on a kind of natural acropolis, with the unoriginal name of Machine Gun Hill. This was situated in the middle of the bowl which contained the rest of the station buildings and a 'township' of three or four Somali shops. The signallers were responsible for the operation of the heliograph equipment and a very cumbersome wireless apparatus. The heliographs looked (and probably were) identical with those used in the Boer War. To me, they seemed very familiar, for I recalled as a small boy studying dramatic pictures of them flashing messages from kopje to kopje in an illustrated, glossy magazine called 'With the Flag to Pretoria'. A complete series of this magazine had lain in a window seat-cum cupboard in the drawing room of my childhood home in Ireland, until the magazines disintegrated with damp and mould. The wireless transmitter was an early model too and keeping it in working condition was a fulltime job. In its appearance, however, it was in advance of its time for it looked like a cross between an electronic computer and a fortune-telling machine.

Daily heliograph contact, through a relay unit stationed on a peak of Labur known as Signal Hill, was kept with a detached platoon that manned the romantic but not very defensible, mud-walled Fort Wilkenson at Todenyang on the Lake shore. The normal officer establishment of the KAR Company was three: a captain in command and two lieutenants. A weekly convoy from Kitale supplied the garrison. The Company's mobility was provided by a fleet of six-wheeler Thorneycroft and Albion trucks fitted out as troop carriers, to a design which seemed to have been based on the old-fashioned Irish jaunting-cart.

The chief pleasure of Lokitaung, as a station, was a small but deep swimming pool which an enterprising C.C. Troops, Captain (subsequently Brigadier) Channer, had constructed some years previously. This he had done by constructing a low, stone wall across the lip of a cavity made by a small stream which tumbled over the side of a cliff into the gorge below. He had then scooped out the debris accumulated through the ages in the huge pothole formed behind it. At this place, those of us who happened to be in the station foregathered in the afternoon. We were usually joined by a small flock of friendly ducks which were the KAR's special pets and jealously guarded from harm. I regret to say that diving competitions for the ducks off the edge of the pool were popular but as it never discouraged them from turning up, they presumably disliked it less than might have been supposed from their indignant squawks.

While I was in Lokitaung, a new commanding officer, Colonel Mundy, took over the 4th King's African Rifles and he subsequently arrived at the station to inspect our Company. The usual spit-and-polish went on for days beforehand and the presently universal whitewash, liberally splashed around, rendered the drab little station almost gay. The colonel arrived late one evening and when he retired to bed immediately after dinner, it was to find a trembling orderly with an ashen face. Eventually this orderly was persuaded to tell the worst. He had forgotten to pack the Colonel's mosquito net, toothbrush, pyjamas, clean uniform and khaki stockings. I soon made good the first three items. The next morning, with a degree of aplomb I have never seen surpassed, he inspected the Company on ceremonial parade tastefully dressed in a most ill-fitting borrowed tunic, a beautifully laundered pair of orange-tinted, corduroy shorts and a pair of multi-coloured, golf stockings. The askari passed him off as some especially exotic Scotsman.

Figure 15: (top) Lokitaung: The District Officer's house and office (at back), (bottom) Lokitaung: the swimming pool on the gorge's edge. Denis McKay on the right.

Not long before the beginning of the Second World War, it was decided that the KAR should conduct their business in English. Up to this point, the official *lingua franca* of the regiment, whose askaris were drawn from many different tribes speaking different languages, had been Swahili. The move was received gloomily by both officers and other ranks of the Lokitaung detachment, especially by the former who were expected to spend so many hours per week giving afternoon and evening classes; and by the senior NCOs who reckoned that their brains had become too solidified to learn any new tricks. It was with great relief and joy that the latter discovered they already knew quite a lot of English, having previously been under the impression that 'stand at ease', 'right turn' and other military commands were Swahili expressions.

Towards the end of one of the earlier afternoon English classes, the instructor became quite desperate and finally asked his blank-faced pupils to say something in English – anything would do – to his nearest neighbour. Deathly silence reigned for a prolonged length of time. Then a bright, young Corporal turned to the stern, bullet-headed Nubian Company Sergeant with thirty years service and ten yards of medal ribbon sitting next to him and remarked, in the most polite of tones: "Hello, darling". On being asked by the startled instructor where he had picked up this expression, the corporal modestly explained that he had been an orderly at Government House, Entebbe (Uganda) for five years and this was what the Governor used to say to his wife when he came down to breakfast.

Life for the askari was happy enough at Lokitaung. They had excellent rations of food, a reasonable amount of work, plenty of organised, if somewhat rough and ready games, with regular changes of scene and occupation when they went out on frontier patrols. And they had their families with them if they were married. We had one tragedy, the first but not the last of its kind with which I have been concerned and one which affected me deeply at the time and for long afterwards.

One Saturday night in the Officers' mess, we had been discussing Company personalities. One of the names which came up was that of a very intelligent, sober and hardworking young askari. He was regarded as the bright boy of the Company and likely to receive rapid promotion. I was awakened at 5.30 next morning with the news that this young man was missing from his quarters. From a letter he had left, it seemed probable that he had gone off into the bush to commit suicide. We later found him hanging from the branch of a small tree not far from the station, carefully dressed in a clean white kanzu. There was a small lamp on the ground below him, the flame of which was still flickering on the page of an open Bible. I do not think it was ever discovered what had led him to take his life. It must have been some unfathomable personal grief that led him to that lonely spot during the night, to enact that so tidily and so carefully arranged drama – perhaps just at the moment we were foreseeing for him an exceptionally successful army career.

Perhaps all suicides are inexplicable and that it is this utter inexplicability which pushes one over the edge. Ten years later, when I was then stationed in the Nandi District, a leprosy survey was being carried out. At one centre, amongst several hundred men who were lined up with their shirts off, the visiting medical expert was delighted to find a man with the disease in the very early stages. I say delighted because it was at a time when a new drug had just been proved which today is commonplace enough. In a speech afterwards to the assembled local dignitaries and populace at large, the expert explained that this man was lucky because six months in hospital would be sufficient for a complete cure. That same night the man hanged himself. He was illiterate and left no message. However, his sister explained at the inquest that he had been very worried: he could not think who would look after his cattle during his six months in hospital.

We had an airstrip of sorts some miles out of Lokitaung and had occasional visits from the RAF in their Vickers Vincent biplanes. These pilots were cheerful enough types but had the annoying habit of finishing off our beer and limited fresh food supplies and then glancing at their watches and saying: "We must really be off. Both Jimmy and I have dates in Nairobi tonight and Paddy promised to run Angela out to Fourteen Falls to see them by moonlight." Nairobi then was a small world compared to what it is now; we usually knew Angela and squirmed to the complete satisfaction of these *blasé* men-about-town.

On one occasion, a flight landed when the ground was soft after some rain. One of the aircraft toppled over and broke its propeller, along with a fine selection of other mechanical components. It was estimated that the cost of all the necessary spares and the work entailed in sending and fitting them came to something like £3000 – a considerable sum of money in those days. It was tactfully suggested that this amount should be paid by the DO, Lokitaung (that is, myself) who as director and controller of the 'aerodrome' should not have permitted the landing. My salary at that time was £35 per month and as can be imagined, I took a dim view of this suggestion. Fortunately, I was able to prove that I had sent a telegram that morning giving the state of the ground. In addition, it was eventually and after much argument held to be an unreasonable assumption that I should sit permanently on the airstrip, ready to put up ground signals as and when required. The matter petered out in a wave of ultra-polite correspondence. This episode brought back to me very sharply the feelings of alarm I had experienced at Cambridge University during lectures on Colonial Accountancy. These had been delivered by a steely-eyed, hawk-faced, ex-financial officer, whose facial characteristics were no doubt the result of closely scrutinising vouchers for twenty-five years – 'scrutinising', of course, being an action entirely distinctive from 'looking at', 'inspecting' or even 'examining'. I wondered at the time how any normal administrative officer ever succeeded in drawing any salary at all, so frequent were the occasions on which, as far as I could see, he must inevitably be surcharged.

(2)

Had it not been for the fact that, at Lokitaung, I was my own clerk, cashier, typist, storekeeper and office boy, there would not have been much to keep me occupied in the station. As it was, there was little difficulty in spending much of the time on tour, either on my own or with one of the KAR officers for company.

Our chief concern was the controlling of Turkana movements in the frontier area, collecting up-to-date information on Italian activities on the Ethiopian side of the border and on the movements and intentions of the Ethiopian and Sudanese tribes, endeavouring to give adequate protection to our own tribes' people and maintaining good relations with our Italian opposite numbers across the frontier. All these matters were, of course, closely inter-related.

At a point near the northern tip of the Lake, the boundaries of Kenya, the Sudan and Ethiopia met. The problem was that no one quite knew where this point was on the ground, although, needless-to-say, each party held its own strong views. The tribes, too, had certain fixed ideas about their traditional grazing rights. Just in case things were not complicated enough, by an arrangement with the Sudan Government, we administered an area north of the official Kenya boundary (or, more to the point, north of two possible boundaries), known as the 'Ilembi Triangle', the extent of which was only roughly determined. On the map, one of these boundaries was a lovely, straight line, of the kind which was so frequently and so whimsically ruled across spaces marked 'Here be Elephants' at the time of the scramble for Africa, with the odd mountain thrown in here and there whenever one Power or another wanted to appear magnanimous. The other boundary, known as the 'red line' – merely because it was so marked on our maps and not because of any bloody distinction – was defined as 'such a line as would leave within Kenya the traditional grazing grounds of the Turkana'. At its eastern, or Lake end, the straight boundary was said to run through 'the northern-most tip, of the northern-most point, of the northern-most crest of the Labur Range'. In my innocence, I once attempted to locate this spot on the ground but soon gave up what was a hopeless task.

It had been only two years since the Italians had succeeded in extending their control to the south-west corner of Ethiopia. During the regime of my predecessor-but-one, large numbers of Ethiopian refugees had been admitted to Kenya via the north end of the Lake, subsequently to be dispersed to refugee camps down country. The international boundary at this point, for many years had been in dispute. Its precise position was a matter of real concern to us, for a section of Turkana lived in the extreme south-western delta area. They made their livelihood by fishing and by growing sporadic crops of millet on the marshy verges. In the past, their rights in this connection had been a constant source of friction with the local Ethiopian authorities. We were determined to do our best to re-assert and maintain them as far as the Italians were concerned. To this end, a Kenya Police post (manned by six men from the Lodwar unit) was maintained on the boundary at the site of the old, Ethiopian frontier post to which the Kenya Government had always laid claim. The Italians were annoyed to discover we had beaten them to it and had to be satisfied with establishing a military post just north of it.

My Italian opposite number, for most of the time I was at Lokitaung, was Tenente Diamente, a pleasant and cheerful man. We spent a certain amount of our time delivering polite but vigorous protests to each other concerning alleged frontier infringements. I have no doubt he obtained as much enjoyment as I did from composing these documents in the most lofty, diplomatic language. Flowery phrases, lush compliments and carefully reserved positions flowed from our pens, painstakingly typed on the best and cleanest bits of notepaper we could find. Neither of us could understand much of what the other wrote but we harboured secret thoughts about the stir these masterpieces would create in Rome and London. Neither side received any other satisfaction out of the exercise.

The easiest tribal raiding route from Ethiopia into Kenya

was straight down the Lake shore, so this route was adequately blocked by the small Police post at Namaraputh, supported by the KAR platoon in Fort Wilkenson, at Tdenyang, three miles to the south. West and north-west was the Labur Range and the extensive, mountain barrier around Mount Lorienetom (rising to over 6000 ft) through which ran several passes. Further west, the Lotogippi Swamp, about 1000 square miles in extent (although this varied with the weather), was a fairly adequate bulwark against raiding parties.

The mountain passes were controlled from three main posts at Naramum, Lokitoi and Kamasia. However, these were not permanently occupied. The theory was that, with motor transport, troops could be rushed to these key points as soon as word of a raid, or of an impending raid, was received at Lokitaung. This was usually good enough but not always. A few months after I had left Turkana in January 1939, a devastating raid was made which our forces failed either to prevent or to cut off on its way back across the border. I suffered acute feelings of guilt about this raid, for it must have been a planned operation about which I ought to have obtained some information. A few wireless sets and some fast jeeps would have made a world of difference - but such luxuries were still a long way off in the future.

The trans-frontier tribes with whom we were mainly concerned were the Merille and the Donjiro, the former living astride the Omo River in the delta area and the latter usually in the Sudan. The Merille were always called the Gelubba east of the Lake and I was to have more dealings with them during the coming war years. Both tribes were akin to the Turkana and all three got along quite amicably when they were not contemplating raids on, or actually raiding, each other – for had they been allowed, the Turkana would have been as active raiders as anyone else. From their point of view, it was a rather one-sided business. However, the alternative to suppressing the martial inclinations of our own people would have been perpetual frontier warfare and complete chaos. There would have been a great deal more suffering and hardship for all concerned – spread over an indefinite area. This was the truth but, bound up as we were with the affairs of the Turkana, we sometimes found it difficult to appreciate. We raged at both our limited competence and the necessity to restrain these warriors from carrying any war into enemy territory. In theory, our well-trained troops, machine-guns and motor transport were a great deterrent but, when it came to 'pressing the button', everything happened much too slowly to bring about the intended annihilation of the swift-moving, conventional tribal raiding forces.

(3)

The countryside round the northern tip of the Lake had a fascination of its own. Whether it was to have a meeting with our Italian counterparts, to inspect the Police post or just *en route* for the north-west round the northern tip of the Labur Range across the dry flats of what had previously been Sanderson Gulf, a visit there was always full of interest. The bird life alone made any visit worthwhile for there were usually myriads of sandpipers, curlews, plover, duck, geese, pelicans, flamingo, sacred ibis, storks, herons and heaven alone knows what other less obvious species to be seen. At certain times of the year, the plains bordering the Lake would be covered with brilliantly coloured, carmine bee-eaters. The area was a major junction and resting place for many other migratory streams. To my great regret, I knew little about birds; but even the most ignorant observer could not fail to enjoy the wonderful display they put on for us. More practical joys were the diet of fresh fish and wild duck that one enjoyed in this area which I am sure only those who look goat and mutton in the face three hundred and fifty days of the year can really appreciate. The other great delight was the sensual, smooth shave the slimy, soda-impregnated, lake water gave. In fact, Lake Rudolph is well worth a visit just to experience the ultimate perfect shave.

The shores of the Lake abounded with the petrified remains

of fish and animals and these too, made an evening walk very interesting. Until the 1934 Lake Rudolph-Rift Valley Expedition, I do not think that much scientific attention had been paid to these fossils or to the shell-beds and marine fossils which were to be found on both sides of the Lake hundreds of feet above the existing level of water - and indeed of any level remembered or rumoured in local tradition.

The Turkana fishing community at Namaraputh used methods which may be common elsewhere but which were certainly new to me. A party of men, each carrying a fish trap which looked like an outsize cover for keeping flies off food, would wade out into the reed-filled shallows, form a half-circle, and move shore-wards. As soon as the fish appeared (and the water often seemed to 'boil' with them), the trap would be thrown over them and the fish removed through a hole in the top. The fish would be strung on a line fastened belt-like round the fisherman's waist and then he moved on to catch more. It was a primitive but most effective form of fishing. The skill with which the darting fish were seen and trapped almost simultaneously was uncanny, especially after one had tried to emulate it. Occasionally, a man would trap a single fish so large that it would fill his upturned basket and he would only just manage to stagger ashore with it.

The sand-baked, mud flats which were all that was left of Sanderson Gulf were noted for their permanent mirage. This gave the effect of there being a continuous sheet of water just out of reach, like the ghost of the Gulf's former glory days rising up to confound the observer. On my first trip across the Gulf, I had with me a down-country servant who felt the Turkana heat greatly. His personal opinion of the Lake region could be clearly understood, although usually delivered in a language which was unknown either to me, to the indigenous inhabitants or to the askari.

We had stopped in the middle of the Gulf to cool the lorry engine and he started to complain at great length of a terrible thirst. One of the KAR askari, with a wink to his companions,

THE GLITTERING LAKE

solemnly said that, indeed, they all felt very thirsty. Would he be kind enough to take a bucket and fetch some water for them – handing him a bucket and pointing to what looked like a great pool of clear water some two hundred yards away. The victim was only too willing and to the accompaniment of much nudging and controlled giggling, he climbed down and wandered off, bucket in hand, a lonely little figure in that great expanse of dry, mud flats and shimmering mirage. When they thought the joke had gone on sufficiently long, they called him back and gave him a drink. He continued to growl disbelief for the rest of the journey and added a completely new section to his standard anti-Turkana repertoire.

Below the great mountain ranges, the Lokitaung area consisted of bare, rolling plains, strewn with loose, volcanic larva rubble of different sizes and densities and colours, with rugged volcanic hills and hillocks here and there, all occasionally intersected by the green belts fringing the sand rivers. These sand rivers became short-lived raging torrents for the few days it rained each year. During these few days, they spilled millions of tons of muddy water into the Lake, discolouring it for miles along the shore and out towards the centre.

As a welcome change from much plain-plodding, John Kent and I (he was second- in-command of the KAR Company at the time) took the opportunity of a joint Kenya-Sudan, preliminary Boundary Commission to make a trip onto the forested heights of Mount Lorienetom. It was our excellent intention that we should go over the ground prior to the arrival of the Commission members, so that we could properly advise them on water supplies, camping sites, passable tracks and all those other things that we thought might be useful to be informed about. Unfortunately, as it turned out, all we got for our efforts was a serious ticking-off for having used up so much of the limited water available. However, as this all came up only on our return, it did not spoil our enjoyment of the safari.

The latter part of our journey was beyond the capabilities of camels, so we arranged for donkeys to undertake our transport requirements from Lokolio waterhole in the foothills of the mountain. This was a large pool fed by a seasonal stream which flowed into it down a narrow channel worn into the rock face. By Turkana tradition, this pool was bottomless. We were mean enough to disprove this theory by means of a large stone tied to the end of camel ropes which showed the depth to be some 40 feet – not literally bottomless but in a country where, apart from Lake Rudolph itself, the average depth of any standing water was about four muddy inches, it was clearly something about which it was worth establishing a tradition.

Having travelled on duty by warship, steamer, aeroplane, goods train, passenger train, motor launch, canoe, lorry, car, bicycle, ox-cart, camel, horse, mule, donkey and on my own two flat feet, I definitely put donkeys at the bottom of the class – or lower, because I never even dared to ride one. I admit they do not smell as much as camels nor do they suddenly kick out at you like mules do; nevertheless, anyone who wants them can have them as far as I am concerned. They are thoroughly unreliable, unpredictable and uncooperative creatures. In their own time and in their own meandering ways, they will carry your loads almost anywhere, depending on what you mean by 'load'. After a few days running-in, they do become more amenable but by that time there will only be small bits and pieces left of your load for them to carry; the beer has been burst, you have run out of invective and you have decided that life is too short, anyhow, really to bother. This trip was no exception to the rule, except that we managed to preserve some of the beer right through the preliminary heats.

Lorienetom means 'the hill of the black elephants'; but years of poaching from the three territories had driven most of the remaining, reduced herds from the mountain. Their scientifically graded tracks remained - and it was these we used once we reached the forest area. To arrive, quite suddenly, in cool, green cedar forest after the hot, lava plains and dusty foothills was to be re-born into a new world; we did not rush ourselves to complete our survey. We spent one day climbing down a

THE GLITTERING LAKE

gorge jammed with enormous boulders. Erosion had terraced this into descending steps, with pools and potholes of gin-clear, cold water on each step – some of them

Figure 16: (top) Namaraputh: Turkana fishermen with fish traps, (bottom) Fishermen returning from the evening sortie, near Namaraputh.

quite large and covered with a mass of water lilies. After three years in the tropics, my vivid recollections of the terrors of bilharzia, a water snail-borne disease, had begun to fade; that is to say, as these terrors had been displayed to a visibly paling bunch of would-be colonial administrators by the late Colonel Stammers, our Cambridge lecturer in Tropical Hygiene. In any case, I do not think that even Stammers himself – he who had solemnly warned us to buy our sun-helmets in England rather than on our way out by ship at Port Said, at the head of the Suez Canal, in case we were shipwrecked in the Mediterranean, he whose command of his subject was such that strong men had been known to abandon their chosen career after hearing his first lecture about 'filthy faecal flies fouling food' – not even he could have resisted the temptation to bathe in these delightful natural baths of highly polished stone, filled to the brim with what to us was a gorgeous luxury: sparkling, ice-cold water.

Although one could not say that the district abounded with game, there were usually some to be seen. Oryx, zebra and Grant's gazelle were common on the plains everywhere, with a good many of the regional reticulated giraffe and the occasional lion and rhino. Along the Uganda escarpment, elephant and eland were sometimes to be seen and both Greater and Lesser Kudo were to be found in the Labur range. On the shores of the Lake, near Todenyang, there was a 'pet' herd of Topi which one saw on the roadside. In the crags and crannies of Labur, Klipspringer were numerous - and I frequently stopped to watch their rock climbing exhibitions when descending into the Lokitaung Gorge. Although I spent a good deal of time attempting to shoot guinea fowl, francolin, partridge, sand-grouse (which came in their thousands to Lokitaung and to many waterholes in the desert country on both sides of the Lake), duck, bustard and other edible birds, I was never anything but a very poor shot. Had I not unhesitatingly adopted the most unsporting methods, I would frequently have gone hungry - or at best have been compelled to eat yet another tough goat which was the equally unattractive alternative. Bigger game I could find no joy

THE GLITTERING LAKE

in shooting. I think I shot two Grant's Gazelles whilst in Turkana because the safari was hungry; and possibly three more antelopes of the same species and for the same reasons, during the remainder of my seventeen years in Kenya, most of it spent in well-known game areas. How shooting of this kind can be designated 'sport' I do not know; and how anyone who has once seen one of these most lovely of creatures bleeding and struggling in the dust, shattered by a bullet from one's own rifle, can bear to do it again for fun is quite beyond me. However, anyone who can nevertheless derive fun from bird-shooting has no right to moralise. We saw little game on Lorieneton but one interesting thing we did observe were the tracks of a dwarf rhino, a rare species known to live in the area.

We came down the mountain by the same route we had ascended, so it must have been on another occasion that I found myself at the wrong end of a game hunt out on the Donyiro Hills in the Sudan. We had noticed that there were an exceptionally large number of animals, mostly Oryx, grazing there and we decided to have a closer look. The plains turned out to be not nearly so flat as they had seemed from above. After we had scouted round and through various small valleys and undulations in attempt to reach the right spot, we heard a peculiar noise, very similar to an old-fashioned train on a country line clanking and puffing as it approaches a station. This turned out to be the main herd of Oryx, several thousand strong, which came stampeding wildly towards us around a corner, in a great cloud of dust. There was nothing more to it than that because they swerved off down another valley at an angle to us. It was a frightening moment – one of those times when your heart seems to stop and time to stand still. We were supremely thankful that the great Station Master above had changed the points to guide the train down another line. The straight, needle-sharp Oryx horn has an especially nasty appearance of its own; although on this occasion their captains would probably have just cried 'feet, feet' in this particular loose scrum.

Figure 17: Lily pond on Mount Lorienetom.

CHAPTER THREE

RUMOURS OF WAR

(1)

The 322 miles of slow and grimy travel from Kitale to Lokitaung had never felt longer than they did on the 28th September, 1938. Our arrival seemed much too good to be true as we rolled round the last bend of the road. My brain slowly began to function again as reality jostled me out of my lorry-stupor. Again, I found myself wondering would it be war, or had the Powers, gathered beneath the shade of Mr Chamberlain's umbrella, decided on some formula for the achievement of peace? The world, as was then its settled custom, was waiting for Hitler to speak. He was probably still trying to get his intuition working as the convoy of four six-wheeler Thorneycrofts rumbled and squeaked to a standstill in front of the Lokitaung guardroom.

The six o'clock news had just been turned on as I entered the Mess: "Today, there have been grave and drastic developments," purred the suave BBC voice. It seemed that trench digging in Hyde Park was continuing with increased vigour. We were led to believe that London was safe, thanks to the timely disposition of a number of anti-aircraft guns (1916 vintage, of course, but in our ignorance, we were reassured).

Having listened to the news as seen from London, I was brought up to date on local affairs. The wireless station had been kept open for the previous forty-eight hours, for the anticipated reception of vital and eagerly awaited orders; the only order received so far had been in respect of twenty-two, unserviceable blankets, overdue for return to store. The Namaraputh Police post had been brought up to its full strength of a Corporal and five men. The platoon at Fort Wilkenson was standing-to, or standing-by, or whatever it was that soldiers then did. Section posts had been established at Naramum, Lokitoi, and Kamasia. It had been reported that the Italian garrison at Maji, the area headquarters, had just received large reinforcements, that all Italian outposts other that at Namaraputh had been withdrawn, and that the Merille were being issued with arms.

A fresh case of beer was broached and the Lokitaung garrison settled down to await its impending doom. In those long-forgotten days, it really felt like doom and we had little doubt that it was impending. Just before dinner, a letter was brought to me by a Frontier Scout.

"A Monsieur Torphe, Officier District, Lochitaunge," it began. "En arrivant de Kalam, ou je me suis place, il m'est cher de vous envoier salutations, dans l'esperance de pouvoir un jour vous connaitre personellement – Primavera Amos, Tenente."

"Well, that sounds friendly enough, in all conscience, only we don't know whether he is relieving Diamenti or reinforcing him."

"Anyhow, what are we deciding about the meeting already arranged?"

We chewed over the situation. It was clear that serious discussion of this problem could be postponed no longer. If war broke out, the 2nd October was generally held to be a likely date, and it was for that date that we had arranged a meeting with the Italians at Namaraputh.

It was largely a matter of National Prestige: if we were to cancel the meeting now, would not the Italians think that we were scared; or that, alternatively, we had inside information? We discussed the question at some length and we almost persuaded ourselves that on our decision depended the whole outcome of the Munich talks. We reached the stage of almost believing that news of any withdrawal on our part, now, might be sent direct to the Duce, who would then feel himself free to take a strong line, as the British were obviously in a state of abject terror. The burden of our responsibility lay heavily upon us.

"On the other hand, if war should be declared and we go to Namaraputh without knowing it, it will mean we all go straight into the box."

"Why shouldn't we put them in the box? Anyhow, war probably won't be declared."

"Because we are under strict orders not to cause any provocation – and if we take an unusually large escort with us that will definitely count as provocation."

Silence fell as we considered this point. It would be bad enough to give indirect encouragement to the Dictators, but how terrible, how utterly devastating, was the thought that, through lack of imagination, we ourselves might be the immediate cause of Global Disaster.

"Oh hell! Let's go. We can take the whole ruddy company and call it a Guard of Honour for old man Primavera, 'en arrivant de Kalam.' That can't be called provocation."

"Can't do that. Any such movement from Lokitaung would require the sanction of God knows who – possibly even the King himself. Anyhow, we can't just abandon the place – it would cause a frightful upset, apart from being extremely foolish."

The soldiers were becoming unnecessarily professional. Nerve-wracked, we retired to bed with the problem still unsolved.

It is now history that on the 29th September 1938 'Peace in our time' was achieved, amidst great rejoicing. In common with most of the rest of the democratic world, we were in high spirits on the 2nd October as our lorries bounced along the track from Fort Wilkenson to Namaraputh. The waters of the lake shimmered in the morning glare and, in the distance, the mirage danced and dazzled across the baked mud of Sanderson Gulf. An arrow of geese, high above us, pushed northwards with the relentlessness associated with bearers of good tidings and joy.

The Kenya Police Corporal at Namaraputh saluted smartly as we drew up outside his little, wired post. As the most northerly representatives of Britain's armed might, who had successfully and unostentatiously kept the frontier inviolate throughout the recent crisis, the six policemen looked surprisingly normal and unconcerned. The Corporal, indeed, remarked that it was over a fortnight since they had received any dates with their rations - and that his men were beginning to think it a bad show. No, he had not seen any Italians for a long time. No, he had not received any message from them about the meeting today. Yes, the Italian post was still occupied and a fresh detachment of Banda[2] had arrived a few days ago.

The leaves on a solitary Dom palm rattled and short gusts of wind blew the sand low along the ground, stinging our bare legs. Suddenly, and for no obvious reason, the atmosphere of the place felt ominous. Had the Italians even heard that the war was off?

We focused our glasses on the stone-walled Italian post across the sand dunes. The flag
ripped and tore at its halyard, high above the fasces-flanked gateway. A sentry gazed vacantly into the surrounding solitude. What fearful and secret weapons might not those deserted walls be hiding? Almost certainly none – but still, one never knew. We ate our lunch in the old Ethiopian Balambaras[3] hut, built on a soft rocky outcrop near the shore.

At three o'clock there was still no word from the Italians so we decided to call it a day. We left a dozen beer bottles and a note for Tenente Primavera, in honour of the peace of the world and of his 'arrivant de Kalam'; but we were vaguely disturbed. Why had the Italians not turned up, nor sent any message? It was almost the equivalent of breaking off diplomatic relations, surely? We piled into the lorries and returned to our camp beneath the crumbling, rubble walls of Fort Wilkenson.

THE GLITTERING LAKE

It was while we were having tea after a dip in the Lake that we saw the signal. The sudden flash caught my eye as I happened to glance northwards along the shore.

Heliography gone mad was the only explanation. But the helio was a few yards away from us and was certainly not at Namaraputh.

Flash – flash – flash, it went – quite unreadable, but clearly of desperate urgency. Flash – flash – flash. Whistles were blown, and from every corner ran men in various stages of undress, hastily arming themselves. Quickly substituting a pair of shorts for a towel, I seized a rifle and sprang into the nearest lorry. Dust spewed from the tank as the convoy raced for the frontier – a Thorneycroft and Albion, both flat out at 12 mph.

A Lewis gun mounted on the leading lorry wobbled in the hands of the gunner as we bounced over the deep ruts. As we came in sight of Namaraputh, tiny figures could be
seen moving about. No sound of firing came to our ears. Had the Police post capitulated to superior forces? Right down at the water's edge, a running figure approached us, waving. A Frontier Scout - and as he rushed up the gentle slope his ostrich-feather headdress flopped wildly. Was he perhaps the bearer of important tidings, if not the sole survivor of a hard-fought action? We stopped as he drew near, and it could now be seen that he was carrying something under one arm. Yes, he gasped in answer to my shout, everything was quite alright. Yes, the Italians had come soon after we had left. Yes, the corporal had had a brainwave and had tried to signal to us with his shaving mirror. He was glad we had seen the signal. Two large bottles of Chianti were thrust at me, followed by a note. The note read: -

'For the Officer District, Lochitaunge.

Thank you very for your beautiful present that I have received with great pleasure. I have not some works for you to thank, because I am very grateful for your great gentleness and because I have a very little knowing of the English language. But I think you would comprendre my sentiments. Je me permets de vous envoyer un peu de vin. Je regrette beaucoups de ne pouvoir pas jouir, aujourd'hui, de votre gentile invitation, et je ne trouve pas de mots pour m'excuser aupres de vous.

I am your,

Primavera Amos, Tenente.'

Figure 18: (top) Namaraputh Police Post, (middle) guard of honour at Italian Namaraputh, (bottom) Todenyang: Fort Wilkenson.

Figure 19: (top) Lokitaung: Tribal Police types, (bottom) Namaraputh: (L to R) Capt. Morris, Tenente Diamenti, Capt. Whitehead and Sotto-Tenente Medico Segreto.

Figure 20: (top) Lokitaung: K.A.R. in troop carrier, (middle) Lokitaung: K.A.R. lines with Machine-Gun Hill in background, (bottom) Lokitaung: Officers' Mess (L to R) John Keane, John Kent, Desmond Prittie and friends.

THE GLITTERING LAKE

We stopped half-way up the gorge next morning to allow our panting engines to blow off steam. The O.C. Troops lit his pipe. "Of course, it's an undisputed fact," he said "that the ice-creamers over the way have about 300 men to every one of ours. But I wonder if they really have much of this aggressive fascist spirit we've heard so much about?"

"Why?"

"Oh, it just occurred to me that possibly news of 'Peace in our time' did not reach Kalama until yesterday morning, and if so…"

An explosion from the back of the lorry cut him short. It was followed by a slight sizzling noise. I hastily climbed up to investigate. A bottle of chianti had blown its cork and a gentle foam was spreading over my kit, watched by an open-mouthed Tribal Policeman. He had been reduced to a state of such complete immobility that it seemed likely to be only a matter of moments before he turned into a pillar of salt. As I stood there, the second cork went bang. The whole thing seemed to be froth and fizz. I picked up one of the bottles. It was marked 'Made in Italy – for export only.'

(2)

After Munich had been over for some time, we inevitably began to receive the detailed orders on what we were to do. These were no doubt of great value a couple of years later but for us they were very much what we should have done if what we expected might have happened, had happened. We were, perhaps not unreasonably, a bit cross about it all.

From this time onwards we became very security-minded and we created hell when a lone prospector turned up one day, with all his permits to enter the district in order. He was an Italian and our suspicions were increased when he announced that he wanted to leave the district via Namaraputh. I gave him permission to prospect for whatever it was the he was looking for, but south of the station only and even accompanied him in person on grounds that I was passionately interested in

73

geology. The air fairly hummed with my protests to Nairobi, and with the soldiers' protests to their headquarters in Uganda. I graciously permitted the prospector to send his own protest against us to the Italian consulate in Nairobi. My Somali Corporal, Abdi, swore blindly he was an Italian army officer – he said he knew by the smell and by the look in his eyes. We won in the end and the prospector left for Nairobi, seething with Latin emotion and uttering dire threats against everyone, from the Prime Minister downwards. As things turned out, I think we were probably right.

Then there were the sheep. The newspapers announced with a flourish that Kenya had found a new market for high-grade sheep in Ethiopia. We were told that the first batch (or one of the first) was to be exported through Lokitaung and Namaraputh, to Maji. In due course, several brand-new, red, four-ton lorries stacked high with sheep whirled into the station. Standing on the running-board of the first two were a couple of Hollywood, khaki-clad, knee-booted frontiersmen - black locks streaming behind and one hand shading the eyes as they peered forward into the unknown. We received them coldly. Corporal Abdi swore they were Italian army officers, this time professional intelligence corps men – he knew by the smell and the look in their eyes. But this time we got no change out of our respective headquarters. The lorries roared off down the Lokitaung gorge, the sheep plaintively bleating and the professional frontiersmen still clinging with one hand and peering eagle-eyed into the future. Corporal Abdi sadly shook his head.

THE GLITTERING LAKE

Figure 21: Travel in Turkanaland: (top) camels....., (bottom) donkeys.....

Figure 22: Travel in Turkanaland (top) lorry .... (bottom) ... and car, the Lodwar - Lokitaung road.

Figure 23: Labur Gorge: rock balanced on a slender rubble pinnacle.

CHAPTER FOUR

INTERLUDE

(1)

Going on local leave from Turkana had a special quality all of its own. After a hectic last-minute rush, during which you swore it was not worth it, (and also just swore); and handed-off the last two dozen people who either thought it would be a good idea if you took them with you or else begged you to make some impossible purchase for them (impossible either by its nature or because you were also expected to loan the required finance); and carefully labelled and packed the last of the sizeable consignment of watches you were taking down for repair; and promised the cook you would bring him back a new frying pan to replace the one which had a hole burnt in it (through which he gave you a sullen glare) – well, you then finally decided to drop everything and go. By the time the lorry reached the foot of the Uganda escarpment and began to grind its agonised way up the Nepau Pass, you began to wonder what all the fuss was about and why you had thought that anything in Turkana was of sufficient importance to worry about. As you wound your way along the first shelf to the foot of the Suk escarpment and then very slowly up, with steam hissing from the radiator and with many a horrid slip and shudder as eye-shutting corners were crawled round and perpendicular gradients surmounted, in a manner which would have surprised no more than the makers of the lorry, you gradually began to realise that another world existed which you had forgotten about. As you pulled into Kapenguria with its trees and lawns, its flowering shrubs

THE GLITTERING LAKE

and neat cultivation, you gulped down the clean, thin air and felt, all of a sudden, that going on leave was a very good thing.

Nairobi, in those days, was not the bustling, cosmopolitan city it is now but it was still big enough to strike both awe and terror into the heart of anyone more accustomed to the traffic problems and pace of life in places like Lodwar or Lokitaung. The average citizen had never even heard of Turkana - and while this meant that coming from such outlandish places you carried with you an aura of he-manishness which was not without its attractions - you were also generally assumed to be round the bend. This was useful in that it excused any oddities in your behaviour. It also meant that no one took the slightest interest in anything you had to say, whilst you could work up no enthusiasm for their affairs. For reasons which will be apparent, I spent some of my leave in Machakos, some 40 miles east of Nairobi, and the administrative headquarters of one of the two Kamba districts, where I had been previously stationed. Here, at least, both the Government officials and the European farmers spoke a language which was understandable, and they felt just as little at home with the Nairobi city slickers as I did. The town of Machakos had once been the capital of the British East Africa Protectorate (in the days when you walked from Mombasa to Uganda), the district was a happy one, and it was the home of some very remarkable characters. I came to know one of them very well, perhaps the most remarkable of them all.

(2)

I was very new to Kenya when I had first visited the Hill homestead and I was most desperately anxious to make a good impression. To have lost my way amongst the maze of rough farm tracks and be late for dinner was a bad start; but I felt even this lapse paling into insignificance as well-meant conversation slowly but inexorably laid bare more serious shortcomings. I was a rotten shot. I knew nothing about coffee growing. My knowledge of cattle was limited to being able to distinguish cows from bulls, if they were standing the right way. It was already known that I was a Civil Servant and when I discovered that this ultimate humiliation would have been forgiven if only I had been good at cricket, there seemed nothing left to say.

I had heard that Harold Hill had been a well-known hunter in earlier days. During this slightly painful initiation into his family circle, my eyes were constantly drawn to the bottom picture of a double photograph which hung about the mantelpiece. I felt I had to do something to change the initial trend of the conversation. I cleared my throat.

"That looks like a lion upside down!" I said pointing to it. I immediately felt it was a foolish sort of remark.

"It is a lion upside down," replied Harold. He took the picture off the wall and handed it to me. "There's quite a story to it, too."

In 1913, a few months after Harold had brought his young bride, Florence Corbett, (a Yorkshire lass) to East Africa, he was lion hunting with a lion-fascinated American, millionaire Paul Rainey. Rainey used a pack of assorted dogs – his 'pot-lickers' – to find lion. The dogs would take the scent but not follow, for, like all animals, dogs fear the king of the beasts. Their yapping, dutch-courage antics, however, annoyed lions sufficiently to drive them from cover.

Rainey was particularly interested in the then new science of cinema-photography and it was his ambition to take moving pictures of a charging lion. For this dangerous project, he enlisted the not un-reluctant Harold. After several abortive attempts, the day came when they found a suitable lion lying-up in a dense thicket. The primitive cine-camera was set up in the open some distance away, with Paul Rainey as camera-man and Harold, with his loaded rifle, as guard. The dogs were put into the thicket to drive out the lion and as they got the scent pandemonium broke out. It was not known which way the lion would go but Rainey hoped to get him in the viewfinder for at least a few moments. He gave strict instructions to Harold that he was not to shoot until the lion reached a certain small bush.

Nothing much seemed to be happening and Harold, remembering his newlywed wife at home, asked what was to happen to her if he were killed? Rainey replied that he would give her a pension. There was still no sign of the lion and Rainey asked: "What happens if she marries again?" "Stop the marriage at once!" was Harold's instant reply. Negotiations on behalf of Harold's potential widow were suddenly cut short. A very large lion broke cover, followed by a chorus of triumphant yelps, and charged straight for the camera. Rainey frantically wound the handle but Harold, with the lion in his rifle sights, found he could no longer see the bush which was to indicate the moment to fire. With great bounds, the lion continued to come charging at them. Harold continued to delay pulling the trigger as the lion came closer and closer. Finally, he knew he could delay no longer and fired. The impact of the bullet caused the lion to make a great somersault in the air and drop to the ground, stone dead. Measurements showed the body to be a mere five yards from the camera or about twenty-five yards nearer than Rainey had intended.

This was the first motion picture to be made of a charging lion and, although by modern standards of payment it does not sound much, Harold was very pleased with himself when he pocketed his $250 fee. The 'upside-down' lion above the mantelpiece in the Hill drawing-room was a still from this historic sequence: almost a close-up, it filled a substantial part of the frame. Its companion picture was a shot of the lion as he broke cover, with two of the dogs in the background.

(3)

For the first few years that I knew him, my chief interest in Harold was to try to acquire him as a father-in-law. I found this exercise a little frightening at times – quite without justification, as I was to discover later. It was not so much his reputation with both gun and rifle of which I was in awe (although this, understandably, might have caused me alarm) but rather his complete mastery of an environment which was strange to me, his forthright attitude towards life in general and his quite extraordinary store of physical energy. He made me feel both tired and useless; and if I already felt tired and useless at twenty-five, he obviously would not consider me much of a match for his only daughter.

Harold Hill came to Kenya in 1905, at the age of twenty-four. He took up land in partnership with his cousin Clifford on the slopes of the Mua Hills, in the Machakos District of what was then called the British East African Protectorate. He picked as the site for his first mud-and-thatch homestead a bush covered knoll from which he could look southwards across the game-covered Athi and Kapiti Plains to the snowy peak of the 19000 ft mountain, Kilimanjaro, some 120 miles away. Born in South Africa of English stock – his grandparents had come out with the '1820 settlers' – Harold had served with Nesbitt's Scouts (an irregular mounted regiment) in the Boer War in 1899. Shortly afterwards, he had become a Treasury official in Johannesburg. It took him just a few years to decide that life amongst ledgers and vouchers was not the life for him.

The East African scene was really 'wild and woolly' during the early years of the 20th century. The main source of the Nile had been discovered by Speke only in 1862 and David Livingstone's death had occurred as recently as 1873. Indeed, it was not until 1867, six years after Harold was born, that His Highness the Sultan Bargash of Zanzibar had granted a concession on the mainland which was taken up under Royal Charter by the Imperial British East Africa Company, whose disputes with the rival German East Africa Company were not resolved until 1890. In 1896, the British Government decided finally to put paid to the remnants of the slave trade and to consolidate its position in respect to the headwaters of the Nile by building the Uganda Railway from Mombasa, on the coast, to Kisumu on the shores of that great inland sea called Lake Victoria.

Construction was completed in 1901 and this had the result, amongst others, of bringing Harold to what is now Kenya. In 1902, His Majesty's Government, appalled at the cost of maintaining indefinitely an expensive railway for which there existed, quite literally, no payload, decided to promote 'white settlement' in the mostly uninhabited lands through which the railway ran for the greater part of its 587 miles.

Harold and Clifford now concluded that they should turn their 6,000 acres of land into an ostrich farm. Apart from the land, Harold's assets consisted of little more than a large, South African ox-wagon, a dog and a few chickens. The few African herdsmen and farm hands he engaged were as willing as he could wish but their only equipment for this strange, new way of life was a deeply-embedded, traditional love for cattle, a couple of spears and a cheerful countenance. There was no lack of candidates for such jobs as were going, for the territory had scarcely recovered from the terrible famine of 1898; this is still referred to as the 'Great Famine', from which many East African tribes reckon the dates of important events since then in their calendar-less history.

The Hills called their farm 'Katalembo', the Kamba name for a type of lizard which frequented the area. One of Harold's first acts when he took up residence was to put a clutch of eggs under a hen. This simple event would have been unremarkable had it not been for the fact that, when he proudly took his first visitor to see these initial steps at farming, they found both hen and eggs gone and a large snake – a cobra – coiled up in the nest. It was a difficult place to shoot but giving a foretaste of the confidence he was later to instil into jittery companions in dangerous situations, Harold persuaded the none-too-happy visitor to allow him to climb on his shoulders. Harold shot the snake, recovered the thirteen eggs intact from its insides, found the terrified hen and put the eggs back under her. It was in complete keeping with Harold's lack of bombast that he was never tempted to end the story other than truthfully – no chicks were hatched out.

(4)

Ostrich farming was a profitable business up to the time of the First World War, with a single feather fetching more than £1 each. However, on the slopes of the Mua Hills, lion and leopard were always troublesome, both being very partial to ostrich meat. When they got amongst the corralled birds at night, they caused ghastly destruction. All injured birds had to be destroyed, for being nervous and highly-strung creatures, treatment of gaping wounds and broken limbs was impossible. Eggs and young ostrich chicks were brought in from the plains, the best feathered birds being subsequently chosen for breeding. Years of selection were necessary to produce first-class feathers and it always seemed to be the best birds which got killed. Once a lion or leopard discovered the 'larder', there was no peace for ostrich or farmer until the animal was tracked down and killed.

One morning in 1908, after a disastrous night, Harold and Clifford set off to follow the offending leopard, their only weapon being a single-barrelled, black powder gun. Some five miles away, they found the culprit in a thorn tree (leopards being agile climbers), with a large lump of ostrich meat providing further proof of his guilt. Clifford fired, the leopard fell and an African herdsman who had arrived on the scene rushed in and poked the body with his spear. The leopard did not move but it was not, in fact, dead. When Harold approached, it sprang up and seized his left shoulder in its jaws. Clifford raised his gun to fire again but the gun jammed. Blows with the butt of the gun only further infuriated the leopard and made it tighten its grip on Harold's shoulder. Thereupon Clifford seized the animal's tail and attempted to pull it off; but he let go in the face of vociferous objections from Harold who felt he was the chief sufferer in this unusual tug-of-war. An awkward impasse was resolved by the leopard itself which suddenly dropped Harold's shoulder and made off into the bush. All the two men could find to wash out the wound was the cold tea they had brought for their lunch but it eventually healed.

Some years later, when Harold was buying cattle for the Army during the First World War and miles away from anywhere in the middle of Masai country, he had another and even more unpleasant experience with a leopard. He was some distance from his camp one evening, shooting guinea fowl for the pot when a leopard sprang on him from behind, knocking his shotgun out of his hand. On this occasion, the leopard seized and badly chewed his left arm. Again, most fortunately, the leopard suddenly decided he had had enough and ran away. Having only mules for transport, it was several days before Harold reached a hospital, by which time his arm had turned black and was badly swollen. It was touch and go whether the arm would have to be amputated – this was what the surgeon recommended but Harold refused. Finally, the surgeon decided to take a chance. He opened-up the wound and soaked it for several days in a saline bath. Once again, recovery was complete.

As a result of these and other experiences with leopard, Harold came to be called 'leopard-bait' by his friends, on the grounds that his attraction for this animal was so great that, if he was present on a leopard hunt, the quarry was sure to be found.

Early one morning in 1909, the train from Mombasa (then, as now, the main gateway to East Africa) jolted to a halt at the little Kapiti Plains railway station. President Theodore Roosevelt and his son Kermit alighted. This was the start of the President's famous hunting safari, in the early stages of which Harold Hill took part.

Some time previously, the Hills' ostriches had been attacked and seriously decimated by a pride of lions. On the night following this most unwelcome visitation, Harold perched himself in the branches of a thorn tree which stood in the middle of the ostrich corral, hoping for a return visit. He was not disappointed. Five lions appeared and began to chivvy the precious birds round their enclosure, seeking a weak spot in the thick fence of thorn branches. The birds, understandably, became very agitated and circled about madly, whilst the excited lions jumped and snarled at them from outside. Harold opened fire, shooting four lions dead and wounding the fifth. The four lion skins subsequently decorated the walls of a house in which the President of the United States stayed.

In the light of subsequent events, it seems strange that Roosevelt was genuinely sceptical of his chances of shooting even one lion in East Africa. The party's total bag of 700 head of game was severely criticised at the time, not least by his fellow-countrymen, as being slaughter on an unnecessarily large scale. It was his English friend, Selous (most famous of all the great East and Central African hunters), who had put him in touch with an acquaintance in the Mua Hills. Roosevelt was even more sceptical when he received a letter promising him as many lions as he cared to shoot and 'guaranteeing success', for above all else, Roosevelt wished to shoot a lion. He shot the first of many shortly after his arrival in Machakos.

Harold Hill accompanied Theodore Roosevelt on several hunting trips. Roosevelt was a little disconcerted, at first, to find how much better Harold's eyes were than his own, ruefully remarking on one occasion that not only did "Harold Hill see everything first" but that it usually took Harold some time to make him see it. There was nothing strange about this, for good shots from other lands always find the East African light conditions strange and difficult at first. Roosevelt soon became used to these conditions and Harold considered him an excellent shot.

Roosevelt certainly enjoyed his stay in the Machakos District. Harold vividly recalled how the American would keep them all spellbound round the fire at night, never failing to hold his listeners' interest while he talked on every subject under the sun. Respect and liking were mutual.

"There was much," wrote Roosevelt afterwards, "to remind one of conditions in Montana and Wyoming thirty years ago."

He felt very much at home with these pioneers who reminded him "at every moment of those Western ranchmen and homemakers" with whom he had "always felt a special sense of companionship and with whose ideals and aspirations" he had "always felt a special sympathy". He was greatly interested in Harold's ostriches and, one day when for the first time, he came across cock and hen ostriches with a flock of chicks, one of his African servants called out to him in great excitement "Look Sah! Look! Ostrich! Bull, cow and pups!"

Roosevelt was given the nickname of 'Bwana Tumbo' by his safari porters. 'Tumbo' in Swahili means 'stomach'. The American press somewhat flatteringly translated this name as 'the Portly Master'. On one occasion, he was having tea in the garden and, as the guest of honour, had been given the one and only camp chair, the other guests having to make-do with an assortment of empty boxes. When Roosevelt rose to take his leave, his chair rose with him.

(5)

When Harold Hill was saying goodbye to his Treasury colleagues in Johannesburg, before setting out for the unknown northern wilds, he was subjected to the usual banter about his probable adventures which would culminate, no doubt, in a suitably sticky end. Included in the interminable good advice was the suggestion that, if he should ever find himself in trouble with a lion, he should get down on his hands and knees, grasp his hat in his teeth and fearlessly advance towards it, making a selection of rude noises as he went. Harold asserts that on one occasion he actually thought of following this advice but had not the nerve – any ordinary mortal will agree that he showed plenty as it was. He was walking back to his camp on the Athi River Plains and, hearing a noise behind him, he glanced around, to find he was being closely followed by a large lioness and her two cubs. Harold walked steadily on, not daring to leave the track nor to look behind again. Just as steadily, his unwelcome companions padded quietly after him. The procession continued in this way for about two hours when, for no discernible reason, mama lion decided she had walked far enough and took herself and her two cubs off into the long grass. Harold quoted this incident as being the worst of all his hunting experiences. He said he had never been so terrified neither before nor since. When he eventually stumbled into camp, he had not a dry stitch of clothing on him.

When the First World War was over, Harold returned to his farm and set about its re-development with unabated zeal. He and his cousin Clifford divided the land between them, each setting up on his own. Ostrich feathers were, by fashion's decree, things of the past. Harold tried wheat but it was a failure due to rust and other diseases and he lost heavily. Then he planted coffee and oranges and began to build up his herds of cattle. Lion hunting no longer interested him, save when the occasional marauder got a taste for ox-flesh and had to be hunted down and killed before it devastated the herds.

Harold now had a wife and two children, Norman and Doreen, to provide for. It was a heart-breaking struggle to make ends meet. It was to get even harder as the post-war depression hit East Africa. His high-grade coffee was now hardly worth the picking and, for lack of fencing, his cattle losses from uncontrollable diseases were heavy. To make things worse, successive droughts and locust invasions smote the area. However, hard times are not always necessarily bad times, especially when all one's friends are in the same boat. Harold and his family enjoyed these strenuous years, notwithstanding the constantly raised eyebrows of his bank manager. He looked the future in the eye as fearlessly as he had faced a charging lion and his abundant, restless energy, backed by a deep love for his adopted country, unbounded enthusiasm and an unequalled capacity for hard work, did much to make up for the notable absence of any hard cash.

(6)

When I saw Harold in 1956, at the age of seventy-five, he was thinking of 'retiring'. Three of us were in the sitting room. It was towards dusk. Doreen was in the middle of a crossword puzzle and Florence, my mother-in-law, was making quiet noises of desperation over a complicated game of patience. I was kneeling in front of a dark mahogany bookcase, thumbing through Harold's collection of Africana books. |Now-and-again, I paused to read inscriptions on the flyleaves of some of the books written by famous men who were part of a chapter in East African history now closed and largely forgotten. *'To Harold Hill with best wishes of Theodore Roosevelt, October 20, 1911'.* A year before I was born, I thought, as I pushed *"African Game Trails"* back into its place and stood up, stiffly. I heard the faint sound of a car.

"That's Harold," said Florence.

"At least it sounds as if he has managed to find top gear," remarked Doreen. "Let's go and meet him."

Doreen and I went out on to the long veranda which stretched the length of the house. A red plume of dust in the middle of the coffee plantation, about a mile away, clearly marked the passage of the car.

"What was that last remark in aid of?" I asked.

"Did I never tell you about Father's first car – the old Overland he had in about 1923?"

"I don't think so," I replied, "but I hope it's not apocryphal, like some of the other mean ones about his adventures with cars!" Harold's mechanical ineptitude had always been something of a family joke.

"Well, as you can imagine, father was frightfully proud of his first car," said Doreen, "and prouder still of his first driving licence. Before he knew very much about driving and with his usual enthusiasm, he decided he would take us to the Nairobi Races." She paused, reflecting for a moment. "I don't remember much about the journey there - but I well remember the scene when we arrived. A policeman directed father to reverse into a parking lot. Of course, to have a car in Kenya in those days was quite a thing and there weren't very many even at an event of such social importance as the Races. 'What!' cried father in some astonishment and annoyance, 'you mean you want me to put it in there – backwards? But I can't drive backwards!' In the end, I think the policeman had to get in and do the reversing for him." Doreen smiled at the memories. "Norman and I weren't a bit interested in the races. He and I amused ourselves for most of the afternoon by taking turns behind the wheel and pushing the levers and buttons and pretending to drive. The car had one of those old-fashioned, hand throttles and, in the course of our 'driving', we had pushed this to full on – and left it in that position. When it was time to go, father, as full of confidence as ever, started up. However, with the throttle full on and the engine roaring away merrily, the only way he could keep the speed of the car down was by driving in first gear – the roads in those days were no more than very rough dirt tracks. He just did not know, and could not work out, what was wrong with the car. We remained in first gear for the whole forty-two miles back to the farm! It says much for the old Overlander that it seemed to suffer no real damage. Indeed, it gave us excellent service for another ten or eleven years."

That evening after our dinner and while we sipped our coffee, Harold broached the subject which I knew had been on his mind for some time. He shifted awkwardly in his chair.

"Going to hand over the farm to Norman," he blurted out. He paused as if he wanted to see the effect of his words. "Dash it, I'm getting on you know. Time he was on his own. I'll just keep this house and a few hundred acres to amuse myself." He gazed out into the darkness. "Some nice coffee land here - I'll put in some water so that we can grow oranges under irrigation – and we can irrigate the coffee too," he added.

As we listened, Harold gradually unfolded his new development plan – a plan for the intensive farming of yet another piece of almost untouched, dry, Africa.

I cleared my throat before speaking hesitantly: "But listen, don't you think it's time you took a bit of a rest?"

Harold stared at me in shock. His pale, blue eyes had a puzzled look. "Rest! You mean sit around and do nothing? Do you want to kill me, or what?"

(7)

Harold's so-called retirement took effect shortly afterwards. Four years later, he was still working from morning to night. More new water dams, more new coffee and citrus plantations were established. Additional fencing and irrigation pipelines had transformed acres of scrubby bush land which previously had provided little more than some rough grazing for cattle. The profits resulting from a decade of good coffee prices had been literally ploughed back into the land. At seventy-nine, Harold looked more-or-less as I remembered him when I first met him twenty-three years previously. He was still the very personification of energy and his slight, wiry, scarred frame carried not one ounce of superfluous flesh. Perhaps it is comparatively easy to cock-a-snook at the passing years, if you have more than the normal share of the kind of guts it takes to hold your fire when a lion is charging at thirty miles an hour straight towards you; and of the different kind it takes to preserve clearly your dream of a wilderness made agriculturally productive through every imaginable trial and set-back.

Harold Hill could have become one of the world's most celebrated lion-hunters – even before 1918, he had shot 138 animals – but he had no real inclination to continue in that direction. In 1956, a photographer arrived at the farm one day and announced that he had been especially engaged to photograph Harold and his cousin Clifford (now eighty-two) for a book his employers were publishing in the United States. The photograph was to show them standing together 'with their trophies' - Harold and Clifford having shot over 300 lions between them. It was a very puzzled and bewildered photographer who discovered that neither of the two famous lion-hunting Hills could raise a single lion-skin trophy. He had to possess his soul in patience while a quick reconnoitre of neighbouring farms was made to find something which would suit the purpose of his assignment. Eventually, a fine male lion-skin with a mounted head was borrowed from Harold's son Norman and the resulting photograph left nothing to be desired[4].

CHAPTER FIVE
MARSABIT

(1)

It was while I was still at school in Ireland that the cinemas had featured a popular series of short films called *Adventures in Africa.* These had been produced by those then well-known American travellers and writers, Martin Johnston and his wife Osa. They were designed to make the ordinary cinema-goer sit-up and take notice. The introduction to each episode in the series was the same and it concluded with something like this:

"And finally, we want all you good folks, sitting in your comfortable seats, to understand that all these pictures were taken under the constant and terrible shadow of death."

The Johnston duo had spent some four years on Marsabit Mountain, some 100 miles east of Lake Rudolf, where they lived beside a small volcanic crater lake deep in the forest, called Sokorte Guda (The Big Crater). They re-named it Lake Paradise ("It was just heaven, so we called it Paradise"). Indeed, they continued to use up much of the English language's stock of superlatives in their cinematic descriptions of the Mountain. I discovered that these descriptions were more than justified during my posting to Marsabit; but those who had had their homes on the mountain since about 1906, in one capacity or another, found it difficult to support the Johnston's claim to have discovered the crater's lake in the 1920's. But then Americans did and still do sometimes get very confused between invention, discovery and commercial exploitation; and so lovely Lake Paradise can take an honoured place beside penicillin, the jet engine, radar and various other wonders, all of which any 'knowledgeable' American will tell you either originated in the USA or was first displayed to the eyes of a startled world by one of her distinguished sons, whose name temporarily slipped his memory. (It would have broken Martin Johnston's heart to have seen his Lake Paradise in 1941, degraded to an army 'waterpoint' and with its water content reduced to a few muddy pools. But I and all those living there through the Second World War held firm to the belief that the little crater lake would recover, some day, its former beauty and grandeur).

Marsabit Mountain was like a beautiful rose blooming in a sooty backyard. I felt certain that that was how the Creator felt about it and why He had so carefully cultivated and tended it. The Mountain was a glorious, green-clad island set in a sea of desolation. To the north and north-east of it especially, great rolling waves of black lava rock and rubble broke on its shores and stretched away in the distance for the best part of one hundred miles. At its highest point, the Mountain was about 5,700 feet above sea level and its fifty square miles of lush forest began at about 4000 feet. To the east, 500 miles of almost featureless desert and flat, thorn-scrub country rolled uninterrupted to the Indian Ocean. To the south, the Kaisut Desert lay in the one-hundred-mile gap to the Matthew Range. To the west, the scrub and sand of the Hedad Desert stretched for about ninety miles to Mount Kulal on the south-eastern shore of Lake Rudolph. This land was flat and covered with boulders of basalt rock with here and there low, flat-topped hills rising out of the desert plain. To the north-west of Marsabit Mountain was the Chelbi – a bare, soda-impregnated, sand desert where endless mirages at first fascinated and later infuriated the traveller. To the north was the Dida Galgalla – waterless, barren, inhospitable, as bad as anything found in the world. It was a dead, nightmarish kind of country of loose, black, volcanic stone which stretched for eighty miles towards the distant foothills of the Ethiopian escarpment.

THE GLITTERING LAKE

No wonder then, that no matter from what direction you came, when you arrived at Marsabit, you could only shake your head and rub your eyes, for it seemed an unbelievable freak of nature. As you climbed up, the grasses grew more and more luxuriantly, followed by a belt of bush, before the forest zone began. Further on, there were tree-fringed crater lakes. The air had a wonderful cooling bite to it; and these were real trees and real green grass. And if you arrived at the appropriate time of the year, the rolling grasslands below the forest edge would be a waving sea of wild gladioli. In the early morning, mists would roll up the mountain side, leaving the vegetation damp with dew-like moisture. Instantly, the dirty, bone-shaking journey through that low-country furnace of jagged rocks, sand and scrub was forgotten. "It was heaven, so we called it Paradise". Martin Johnston was perfectly correct about Marsabit Mountain.

(2)

It is not known who was the first European to visit Marsabit - but it was seen in the distance by Count Teleki in 1886 as he journeyed up the eastern shore of Lake Rudolf. Of this land, Von Hohnel later wrote in his book: 'Into what a desert had we been betrayed! A few scattered tufts of fine, stiff grass rising up in melancholy-fashion near the shore were the only signs of life of any kind. Here and there, some partly in the water, some on the beach, rose up isolated skeleton trees stretching their bare, sun-bleached branches to the pitiless sky. No living creature shared the gloomy solitude with us. To all this was added the scorching heat and the ceaseless buffeting of the sand-laden wind, against which we were powerless to protect ourselves on the beach, which offered not a scrap of shelter.'

In 1897, Lord Delamere, with Dr Atkinson, passed through Marsabit on a journey down from British Somaliland and eastern Ethiopia. He had camped by a small spring which before the Second World War was the sole water supply for the village and Government station and which came to be known as Delamere's

Njoro. The American explorer, Dr Donaldson-Smith[5], had also passed by Marsabit a year before Delamere.

Until the outbreak of war, the normal white adult population of Marsabit District was a minimum of two and a maximum of four – two if the District Commissioner and the Police Officer were bachelors and four if they were married. Up to that time, it was the only Kenya frontier station to which officers' wives were allowed to accompany their husbands.

The principal tree in the Marsabit forest was the brown olive and, except near the summit, the timber was not large. The trees were all lichen-covered and this gave a very motheaten appearance from a distance. There were no palms and few ferns. Balsams were plentiful and at certain seasons of the year, the forest floor was carpeted with red and white lilies. Few of the forest birds one might expect were to be found, not even the larger hornbills and green pigeons. In March and April, however, several European migrants arrived – great flocks of swallows would suddenly appear and also sand martins, sedge warblers and chiff-chaffs. Insect life was abundant, some pleasant like gorgeous butterflies and some very unpleasant such as jigger fleas and a large variety of ticks. After the rains, clouds of butterflies would appear and these were one of the unique features of the mountain. There was a rumour current during the War that these butterflies were worth £1 each in the USA. Their numbers were so great that had they been worth a penny a dozen they could have just about paid for the War – and left quite an amount over for the development of the District.

The real lords of Marsabit Mountain were the elephants, who frequently pushed their way into the District Commissioner's garden or scratched their enormous itches on the corner of his house. A stroll along the forest edges was often rewarded by the sighting of a greater kudu (a large antelope) and giraffe on the roadside almost ate out of one's hand. At the quiet forest pools, a great variety of wild animals came to drink. A favourite evening stroll was to a small, reed-filled crater called

Sokorte Dikka (the Small Crater), some fifteen minutes walk from the District Commissioner's house. Here, more likely than not, elephant, rhino and buffalo would be seen drinking in the cool of the evening. Further away and below the forest, a very large sunken crater called Gof Bongole (a mile or more in diameter and several hundred feet deep) was the place to view elephant *en masse*. Frequently, elephants shared the water in the open pools at the bottom of the crater with the local cattle. I have observed myself the elephants hanging about in the nearby undergrowth while the cattle drank and then, as the herd boys drove out their cattle, the elephants would start simultaneously to move down to the water. It was all a very friendly arrangement with the rules well-known and obeyed by all parties.

(3)

Five tribes inhabited the 26,000 square miles of the Marsabit District and, at the time with which this book is concerned, all five tribes totalled under 27,000 people. About a square mile per person may sound a reasonable allotment but in a countryside which could on average carry possibly one goat to fifty or sixty acres and where cattle could sometimes be watered only once in every three days (and spend two of these walking to and from the water) it was not all that generous.

The Boran and Gabbra tribes were of Galla stock, speaking the same language and originating in southern Ethiopia, where the main body of the tribe still lived. The Boran were cattle people and lived on the slopes of Marsabit Mountain, whilst the Gabbra counted their wealth mainly in camels, sheep and goats, living in the desert country to the north and north-east. Both tribes being nomadic, their whole life was bound closely to their livestock. However, due to the comparatively very much easier conditions on the mountainside, the Boran's existence was already becoming semi-nomadic and a few of the families had even begun to try their hands at a traditionally unheard-of occupation – agriculture.

The Rendille who lived to the west and south of the Mountain, were a tribe of mysterious origin. It seemed that the tribe was of Somali stock and spoke a language which has been described as a kind of archaic Somali. Tribal tradition had it that they had moved down from the Horn of Africa; but it was so long since they had left their reputed homeland that they were now pagans with only the smallest trace of Islamic customs. To the Europeans, the Rendille had always seemed a more friendly, simple, manly and amenable tribe than their Galla neighbours. Their general outlook was, of course, influenced by the fact that they did not have the trans-frontier interests and allegiances of the Boran and Gabbra tribes. Like the Gabbra, they were true nomads and their wealth, which was vast, consisted of enormous herds of camels, sheep and goats.

Like the Turkana, the male adults of all three tribes were obliged to pay an annual poll tax but in contrast to the Turkana, this tax had to be paid in hard cash. This was fixed at ten East African shillings per man (compared to the Turkana three shillings) but even at this rate it meant nothing to them financially. Like all such obligations, it was just a bore. It was also a great nuisance for those of us who had to collect it because the Revenue Office in Nairobi had designed a special Northern Frontier District Poll Tax Receipt. Naturally, this had to be prepared in triplicate. I do not suppose any of the designers had ever tried to handle two carbons in a sixty miles per hour, sand-laden gale. There was no doubt that catching Turkana goats was much more fun for everyone.

On the south-west shore of Lake Rudolf lived the Elmolo tribe, (in Galla, 'poor devil'), chiefly distinguished for the number of learned anthrop-and other-ologists who came to study them from time to time. In 1940, they numbered only some eighty souls, the survivors of the earlier fishing population of Lake Rudolf. The Elmolo lived entirely by fishing and had only just been saved from complete extinction. For an allegedly dying race, I always found them to be quite remarkably cheerful. They were consciously proud of their position as persons to whom some special importance was attached, without any clear idea of what this special importance was. They themselves claimed to be a distinct tribe but it would seem much more likely that they were the concentrated remains of the low-caste fishing sections of the earlier Samburu and Gelubba (Merille) tribes when the former penetrated further north and the latter further south and possibly also of the Rendille. This, at any rate, was the view of Von Hohnel who recorded their number at five hundred when he and Count Teleki met them in 1888. The number counted by the Lake Rudolf – Rift Valley Expedition in 1934 was eighty-four. They also recorded a view commonly held in Marsabit, namely that one factor in the preservation of the tribe had been the presence of a King's African Rifles outpost at Loiyangolani during the period 1910 – 1917. The assistance rendered by the soldiers, many of whom probably belonged to tribes bordering Lake Victoria, included some mixture of blood and the provision of iron for fishhooks and harpoons. They may also have taught them how to make and use fishing nets (which they now made beautifully and used very skilfully), for according to Von Hohnel, they did not possess nets in 1888[6].

At the north-east corner of Lake Rudolph, in the eastern delta area, lived a section of the Merille. This group straddled the Omo River (the only river flowing into the Lake) and who, on this side, just to make matters more difficult, had always been called the Gelubba. Up to the period of the Second World War, both they and the Kenya territory in which they lived were un-administered. As far as Marsabit District was concerned (and in Turkana on the opposite shore) the Merille were very definitely 'the enemy' – and a very real enemy, too.

In the little Marsabit Township, there lived in small numbers, a conglomeration of tribes. The only ones to reach double figures were the Burji and Konso, agriculturalists from a group of tribes always referred to as Ethiopian slave tribes. These had been admitted from across the Ethiopian border specifically for the purpose of cultivating the fertile soil which no proud nomad would deign to touch. They were industrious people who prized highly the cultivation rights given to them. When sober, they were most worthy citizens.

(4)

Such, briefly, was the Marsabit District to which I was posted as District Commissioner in late1940 – geographically vast, extremely arid, sparsely populated and dominated by its mountain oasis. The name 'Marsabit' implies a 'good place, cold, misty and with trees'. It was certainly good to stand on one of its mountain peaks in the cool of the evening, with the closely packed forest lying beneath your feet and the seemingly endless desert, for all the world like an open sea, stretching out on all sides to the hazy distant hills that shimmered and danced in the desert air still hot from the passing day. No young DC could view the prospect unmoved, for here he was, in truth, lord of all he surveyed. It could make him feel humble or arrogant, according to his nature - but it could scarcely fail to fire even the most turgid imagination. It was only when he moved out into the desert plains and felt himself wilt under the scorching sun and the burden of frustration engendered by his growing knowledge of the fact that his chances of ever achieving anything very constructive were small, that the rosy light of youthful fervour would begin to show distinct signs of flickering.

Only my predecessors knew the District in its heighday, for the Second World War had started by the time I arrived and almost a third of the area was under enemy (Italian) control. Not indeed that anyone had ever looked out from such a mountain peak on anything but a battlefield; for the tribes had always had to fight for their very existence: for their right to take their camels to a certain waterhole, for the right to certain grazing areas. It was a very tough country and only the tough survived.

(5)

Places like Marsabit District (and they comprised a goodly proportion of the Earth's surface) would be uninhabitable were it not for that remarkable and often unnecessarily maligned animal, the camel. This animal must surely come high on the list of mankind's greatest benefactors. I do not know the record length of time for a camel to go without water - but I recall eight to ten days as being nothing remarkable. Whilst his ability to do this is his chief asset in a waterless country, his ideas on what is delectable in the food line runs it a close second. A camel's mouth with its apparently soft, fleshy lips, appears so tender that you can but stand and stare in amazement when, for the first time, you observe him browsing in ecstasy on a fearsome thorn tree like the 'wait-a-bit' (aptly so called because its curved thorns are set at all angles and capture your clothing or body if you as much as brush lightly against it). A camel will chew off or strip the branches of this and other thorn trees with the most obvious enjoyment.

If you possess a reasonable number of camels, you have everything required to support human life. You can live on their rich milk (fresh or curdled); and you have camel meat to celebrate those special occasions in a nomadic family's life. In addition, you can make your clothing, your tents, your water and milk containers, your ropes and your harness from their skins. Camels will transport your tents when you move on to new grazing areas, your belongings, your family and, if necessary, yourself according to the seasons. Most important, they will carry water for the journey without using any of it for themselves. 'This, gentlemen, is the camel ...' It could, with a great deal of truth, be re-written: 'This gentleman (or lady) is the camel'.

The Rendille recognised eight types of camel, according to their colouring. The gestation period for the female camel was thirteen months and it was said that when on the rare occasions that twins were born, the male camel became very upset. While the milking of sheep and goats was the work of women, it was the men who milked the camels. The life of a camel was put at thirty years.

The traditions of the Rendille were very closely bound up with their camels and some of their customs were very complicated. For example, if I gave you a camel, I could say, at the same time, that it was only for the milk - although I might leave the camel permanently with you. In that case, every female calf would be mine and would be marked with my brand and every male calf would be yours and so would carry your brand. On your death, you would bequeath the camel and her progeny to your son and the process would continue even, even on my death, through my son: females to my sons, males to your sons. This system could continue for generations and both male and female camels would all still be kept by you. If in a fit of temper, I were to go and collect all 'my' camels from you (or my descendents were to do this to your descendents), the tribal elders would probably order all 'mine' be returned to you, while still recognising that they were legally mine. As you can imagine, claims based on this custom usually required a lot of sorting out.

The traditional punishment for stock theft within the Rendille tribe was that the thief must re-pay three times what was stolen i.e. three camels for one stolen camel. However, anyone in any way connected with the theft in a very wide definition of accessory before and after the fact was deemed also to be the thief and was obliged to pay three camels for every one stolen. For example, if two men were found eating the stolen meat and ten others, say, joined them round the fire, then all twelve could be held liable, even though the ten had done nothing more than stoke the fire. The Rendille reckoned this to be a very efficient deterrent system, as even the boldest would hesitate to have anything to do with an animal or its meat if it could be even vaguely suspected of being stolen.

At the start of a camel journey, the baggage camels could be very troublesome. However, I only ever experienced one camel which uncompromisingly refused to walk in the familiar string, single file, head to tail. This camel was a handsome, white beast. While not refusing to carry a load or to walk along quietly, it just would not stay in line and instead insisted on walking at the end of a taut head-rope some distance to the side. Invariably, we would put this individualist at the very tail end of the safari train. During some three weeks' walking round Mount Kulal and up the mountain, it insisted on maintaining this awkward position. The camel leader in charge of the section kept tut-tutting, shaking his head and muttering: "It won't lead and it won't follow but just wants to wander about like the elephants of Losedan." I enquired about these elephants but he was unable to tell me anything more about these apparently notorious beasts. As Losedan was a well-known swamp, I assumed there was some moral to the story in which they all came to some sad and appropriately sticky end on account of their stubbornness.

(6)

North and slightly west of Marsabit Mountain and a little south of the Ethiopian escarpment lay a volcanic mountain range called the Hurri Hills, rising to about 4,000 feet above sea level. They were practically treeless and had no permanent water. After the rains, they would be clothed in lush Red Oat grass and were a favourite wet-weather grazing ground of the Gabbra. While cattle could only remain there a short time because the rainwater pools soon dried up, their sheep and goats (which could survive without water almost indefinitely so long as they had fresh, green grazing) stayed on much longer. The upper regions of the Hurri Range were cold and windy; some of the nights I spent there were as cold as any I have spent anywhere. It was almost impossible to find any shelter from the everlasting gale which at times was so strong that it was physically impossible to pitch a tent. To say there was no permanent water is not strictly correct - in one location there was a minute spring which just wetted the ground - and which could produce, perhaps, a few bucketfuls per day. On one occasion when I arrived to camp there in the dry season, the little spring was packed solid with thousands of small birds, each trying desperately to reach the water. Hundreds had already died or were dying; the living birds took not the slightest notice of the presence of human beings.

We made several attempts to construct earthen reservoirs in the Hurri Hills but with little success for the volcanic soil was too loose and porous. We did manage to make one reservoir to hold water for a while - but it was too small to be of much value. It did, however, demonstrate that, with perseverance and greater skill (and with more money), the development of this large and important grazing area was possible.

The other main hill feature of the District was Mount Kulal, situated just off the toe of Lake Rudolf. This mountain was quite different from both Marsabit and the Hurri Hills. Much of the top of Mount Kulal, which rose to about 7,500 feet above sea level, was covered with cedar forest (which unfortunately suffered periodic fires which we could not control). Other parts consisted of the most attractive parkland with broad, green glades dotted about with clumps of trees. When I sat at the top of the mountain, surrounded by this lush vegetation and looked westwards over the blue-green water of Lake Rudolf, I found it hard to believe that I was not in some part of the Kenya Highlands, north of Nairobi, or even perhaps in the British Isles. The sight of the camels peacefully browsing nearby produced the same feeling of incongruity as would the sight of a camel on Hampstead Heath. A strange feature of this range was the enormous crack which ran through it from east to west, a 3,500 feet deep and narrow gorge which split the mountain in half from top to bottom.

On the west side of Mount Kulal, a wonderful, clear stream ran down into the Lake at Loiyangolani, slightly north of which were the hot springs at Hadad. People who were sick and ailing sometimes travelled hundreds of miles 'to take the waters' which tasted of pure magnesia. It is probable that it was at these springs that Count Teleki camped on the 12th March 1888. He records that the air temperature was 32^0 C whilst the temperature of the water was 42^0 C. I once departed my campsite at 3 a.m. with a very chilly breeze whistling in off the Lake - a couple of buckets of hot water to wash in were a very welcome luxury.

Marsabit, Kulal and the Hurri Hills were all substantial mountains, each rising to over 4,000 feet. However, there were also other impressive but lower, hill features east of Alia Bay, situated on the east shore of the Lake, namely Derati Hill and a high lava plateau known by several names, one of which was Algole. In search of a suitable line along which to construct a strategic motorable track to the north of the Lake, I once did a rapid tour of the plateau area. This had sheer sides rising to about 2,200 feet above sea level or 1,000 feet above the Lake. I could find no one in my safari that had ever been up it or knew anyone who had been up it. After scouting around for some time, I saw what looked like a possible but difficult route. Clearly it would be hard going with loose larval rock in all kinds of grotesque formations. When I pointed to the 'path' I had selected, at least four voices immediately announced that, of course, they knew the area well and it was quite impossible to find any route which the safari could safely ascend. After reaching the top with much difficulty, we seemed to be standing on an extensive, flat plain. As we travelled on, it soon became apparent that the whole plateau country was divided into blocks by deep gorges so that it was not one single, extensive plateau but a series of flat-topped hills all at exactly the same level. However, when we turned towards the Lake we could see other sets of flat-topped hills at lower levels so that the general land formation looked like the following diagram:

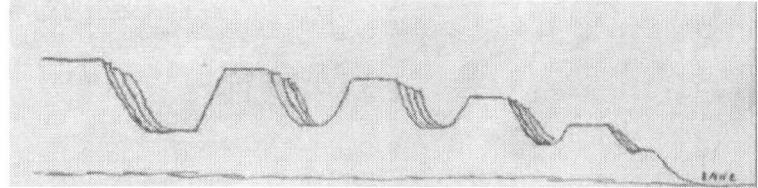

On a previous occasion, I had walked through the black, tangled volcanic slagheaps nearer the Lake at Kubi Fur, north of Derati Hill and found a great number of shell beds. Some of the shells were in a petrified state and others just old but still in perfect condition. There were also masses of petrified bones the same as I had been familiar with on the lake shore at Todenyang on the opposite side. I was not surprised to see these at first but when I continued to find them up to a height of 300 feet or more above the existing lake water level, they suddenly became more interesting. At the time when the Lake was at such a height, a vast area of land must have been under water and one would have expected to make similar finds very much further afield. I certainly never did - and I always had my eyes open for anything that might add to the interest of lengthy and often very boring walks; of course, not having made such finds did not mean they were not there. At that time, I had not read Fuch's opinion, following his 1934 expedition, which is that the evidence of human culture in the Lake deposits makes it seem probable that the greatest spread of water was attained during the lower part of the upper Pleistocene period, some 100,000 years ago. The evidence of the old lake beaches also shows that its surface once lay at least 350 feet higher than at the present; and, also, that at some occasion it had been at a lower level than at present. He concluded from the evidence he found in the hills to the north-west of the Lake that the Lotogippi Swamp was once joined to it and that the Lake's outlet across what are now the plains between Mount Lotienetum and the Donyiro Hills wound into the far north-west to form a link with the Nile system[7].

THE GLITTERING LAKE

(7)

I always found it an enthralling experience to be near a large Gabbra or Rendille encampment in the evening when their flocks of sheep and goats were returning from the grazing grounds for the night.

On one safari, I had with me a young, newly-appointed Kikuyu tax-clerk whose home was near Nairobi. Many people without any knowledge of Africa are inclined to assume that all Africans, by nature, must be at home in the bush and to have had a life-long acquaintance with big game animals. But there are today probably many millions who may never have seen even the commonest type of antelope and who know as little about 'life in the wilds' as any Cockney. Certainly, Jonathan Kamau was a real 'townee' and, needless to say, he had his leg pulled unmercifully by the other members of the safari. Not that it was all leg-pulling, for although his terrified reaction to seeing, suddenly, a giraffe peering at him over the top of a thorn tree almost broke up the safari so great was the general merriment, he really had some cause for alarm a few nights later when a leopard leapt over his camp bed and seized a goat which was tethered to my interpreter's bed just behind him. This incident almost ended in tragedy because Jonathan jumped out of his bed and bolted into the darkness. We spent most of next day looking for him and, when we eventually found him, he was in the last stages of exhaustion.

Jonathan attempted to make up for his lack of bush lore by throwing a big line on education, trade and, in general, the superior wealth and sophistication of the Kikuyu tribe. In line with many of his fellow-tribesmen at that time, he despised the nomadic peoples of the Northern Frontier as uneducated savages.

One afternoon on this particular safari, we were heading for a large Rendille encampment in the northern Hedad. Jonathan was in full tongue on the superiority of the Kikuyu. Like so many other people, he too readily assumed that anyone who wore skins or just a simple cloth, who usually travelled on foot and who was frequently covered with dust and dirt, must also be very poor. Two Rendille tribal Policemen were listening very politely to his glowing account of his own people and their way of life. When he paused for breath, one of them asked:

"Tell me, Jonathan, do the Kikuyu have any stock?"

"Oh, yes, indeed," replied Jonathan, puffing out his chest with pride, "some of them have as many as fifty cows and most have at least two or three!"

"Um – I see, and have they any sheep or goats?"

"Oh, yes," said Jonathan, "indeed they have."

"Many?" enquired the Tribal Policeman.

"The ordinary person would have five or six, perhaps but some wealthy men have well over a hundred; some have many more."

"Indeed, your tribe is very rich," remarked the Tribal Policeman with a gleam in his eye, "But, of course, we Rendille also have sheep and goats."

"Have you really?" said Jonathan in a rather patronising tone of voice. "I haven't seen them; and anyhow, how can they live in this miserable kind of country?"

"Oh, they live all right," replied the Rendille with a laugh, "but I realise we have difficulty competing with the tremendous wealth of your people." He continued to snigger quietly to himself.

A few minutes later, we debouched from the valley we had been walking along. There, in front of us, beneath some low hills, was the Rendille encampment – a very large one. The light was beginning to fail by now, but the rolling hillocks around us were white.

"Look, Jonathan," said the Tribal Policeman, pointing his finger towards the encampment and surrounding low hills.

Jonathan looked. When he realised that the apparent whiteness of the hillsides was, in fact, flowing rivers of sheep and goats coming home for the night, he literally stopped in his tracks as if he had been shot. His eyes bulged and he gave a gasp. Then he pulled himself together, nodded solemnly and regarded his travelling companions with a new respect.

"Yes," he said finally in a quiet voice, "yes indeed, you Rendille do have some sheep and goats."

By the time we had arrived close to the village, all the various streams and eddies of bleating animals had joined up. The air was solid with their cries and thick clouds of yellow dust arose over us. It was an amazing sight and I do not think that poor Jonathan ever really got over it. There were possibly fifty thousand animals there that evening but I did not try to count them; nor would the Rendille. However, any of the owners could have told us if any one of his animals was missing from those huge flocks.

(8)

The Boran, Rendille and Gabbra all had their traditional areas to inhabit, based partly on recognition of early occupation rights, partly on attempts at a fair division of water supplies and partly on the needs of internal and external security. To the north-west and south, the Rendille had similar relations with the neighbouring Samburu and Boran of the Maralal and Isiolo Districts, respectively. To the east, few problems existed for in this direction there was a large area of waterless no-man's-land, providing quite an effective buffer between the Marsabit tribes and the Somalis of the Wajir District. Only during the rains could any use be made of this land.

The three tribes normally maintained reasonably friendly relations with each other, so much so, that it became all too easy to allow oneself to be lulled into a false sense of peace and goodwill. In time of drought, they would on occasion, jointly ask for approval for an arrangement to share waterholes and out of necessity this sometimes was permitted. The problem was that, however great the expression of goodwill at the start, it only needed some minor incident, such as the theft of a few goats by members of one tribe from members of another, to start a snowball of attacks which could easily develop into outright warfare. The most inflammable incident which could, and indeed did, happen was the killing of a child by a member of another tribe. When this or some other serious incident occurred, any failure to take swift and immediate action, both directly against the offenders and by separating the tribes, could have very serious consequences. War parties from other parts of the District would start moving in and these had to be stopped and sent back to their areas before they joined together for the purpose of launching a major campaign.

It was traditional amongst nearly all the border tribes, on both sides, that when a young man officially reached warrior status, he had to provide proof of his manhood by killing an enemy or at least some dangerous animal such as an elephant, lion, rhinoceros or buffalo. This custom was sound enough in origin and its merits must have been plain when all the tribes were laws unto themselves; when they were surrounded by actual or potential enemies, both human and animal and when the very existence of the tribe depended on the strength and skill of its young warriors. However, it was not a custom which fitted in very well with civilised conceptions of the Rule of Law, the King's Peace, the sanctity of human life, the conception of murder as an offence against the State and the desire of governments to protect wildlife. The custom died hard and one of the unfortunate results was that its form remained – as in the case of other customs of other tribes – notwithstanding the fact that its purpose had ceased to exist. It became debased to the necessity for a token killing only; for this, human male babies and baby elephants had long since been found to be easier victims than adults. While such offences against game were, unfortunately, frequent enough, it was when a young man could no longer bear the taunts of his girl-friend to the effect that he was a sissy that he would, in desperation, set forth and spear the first male child, of another tribe, that he could find. In doing so, he hoped to put his manhood and warrior-status beyond all doubt. The trophy he would return with in triumph was not the scalp (to which Red Indian stories have rendered us so accustomed that we might regard scalping as something quite natural) but the genitalia. The male private parts were the recognised trophies of war amongst the Ethiopian and north-Kenya tribes.

When it came to massacres by raiding parties, it must be admitted that there was nothing, in theory, to choose between any of these tribes - all could be quite ruthless. However, as the tribes in Kenya territory were administered and controlled and so had few raiding opportunities, our hatred was not unnaturally focussed on those who came across the border from Ethiopia. These raiding parties wiped out and mutilated whole encampments and drove off the stock to the immunity of their own wild homelands. I never saw with my own eyes the immediate aftermath of a border raid - but I have heard many first accounts and seen photographs. Some of these incidents were extremely distressing. It was usually, however, carelessness rather than deliberate savagery (unlike, for example, the deeds of the Mau Mau); and while, it was traditional to mutilate the bodies by cutting off the breasts of women and the genitalia of men, the intention was to kill swiftly and sweep back across the border before any retaliation operation could be mounted. If it should happen that a speared child was picked up alive a few days later, half eaten by ants, the moral position of the killer was somewhat akin to that of a western bomber crew – fundamentally, perhaps it could be argued, rather better.

(9)

When Count Teleki trekked up the eastern shore of Lake Rudolf in 1888, the whole country in that region appears to have been teeming with wild game of all kinds, including vast numbers of elephant and rhinoceros. Herds of elephants came down to the Lake to drink and bathe and Von Hohnel's narrative is punctuated with heroic drawings of elephants despatched in the nick of time by the heroic and gallant Count. In one day, close to Alia Bay, the Count shot five elephants with the heaviest pair of tusks weighing some two hundred and twenty-seven pounds. Two days later, on the Lake shore, he shot another elephant whose tusks weighed two hundred and thirty-six pounds.

Between the 6th and 30th March, 1888, while his safari was moving slowly up the Lake shore, the Count's personal bag of game included ten elephant, seven rhino, two buffalo, one leopard, three hippopotami, four zebra and two Grant's gazelles (which latter he apparently brought down with a single shot). Elephant and buffalo on the Lake shore were almost unknown long before I arrived in the area; hippos were not very plentiful and there was only the occasional rhino. Thus, in less than forty years, the big game animals had been almost wiped out around Lake Rudolf. All the same, I encountered my first rhino near Derati Hill and I remember it very well. We were grinding slowly down a slope in our truck and, for some reason, I was the only person to notice the animal standing under a thorn bush just beside the rough track. It looked at us with an expression that seemed to me to be full of belligerent intent. I shouted to the driver what was the local equivalent of 'step on the gas.' With the noise of the engine that was grinding in second gear, he did not hear me correctly and assumed I had asked him to stop – which he did with a sudden jolt, almost opposite the rhino's horn. Fortunately (as no doubt the good Count would have said and as I felt), the chattering crew on top of the truck let out a unified shriek of surprise and fear. The rhino, probably equally frightened, turned and trundled off into the bushes at a gentle trot. The driver then saw it for the first time and made the quickest get-away I have ever experienced or seen from a standing start.

The areas for the big game in my time were not out in the desert and by the shores of the Lake but on Marsabit Mountain, Kulal and in the Horr Valley in the south-west; but regretfully I can claim no great adventures. It was commonplace, in peace time, to have elephant in our garden in Marsabit. When I saw one near the house for the first time (when they had returned to the mountain after the War had passed us by), our small kitchen-boy, or toto, was chucking stones casually at it across a shallow gully and suggesting that it went away. On one occasion, sleeping in the open at South Horr, I was awakened for my morning tea by the sound of queer gasps from the servant who, with his mouth agape, stood holding a wobbling cup in a shaking hand. The clear pug-mark impressions of a very large lion showed where he had passed silently during the night just a few feet from my head; thus I missed the chance, as I had been asleep, of being able to say I have seen a lion anywhere outside of a zoo or a National Game Park and this after many years in the wilder districts of Kenya.

Figure 24: Marsabit types: (top) Somali, (middle) District Commissioner's staff outside his office, (bottom) Boran, Arab and Rendille.

Figure 25: (top) Marsabit: the remains of "Lake Paradise", 1943, (bottom) Marsabit: Burji smallholder ploughing.

Figure 26: Loiyangolani: Elmolo family with fish.

Figure 27: On Safari: (top) camp for the daytime, (bottom) camp for the night.

Figure 28: (top) conscientious objector, (bottom) loading camels.

CHAPTER SIX
WAR

(1)

I departed on home leave to Ireland from Lokitaung in February 1939 and returned to Kenya early in August. Doreen and I were married in Nairobi Cathedral on the 26th August. We were on our honeymoon in Mombasa when war was declared on the 3rd September. I had been posted as District Officer to Kwale, a station some 20 miles south of Mombasa and we reported there for duty. Before long, Doreen who had been a peace-time member of the FANY was called up and I was left holding the civilian fort, fulfilling so I was informed 'work of national importance.' It was presumed, not unreasonably, that more of this 'work' was going on in the bustling port of Mombasa than in sleepy Kwale so I was sent back to Mombasa to help. Having arrived there, no one could think of anything for me to help with, important or otherwise. After this situation had been confirmed to everyone's satisfaction, I was duly sent back to Kwale.

In July 1940, I was posted to the Northern Frontier District as District Officer, Isiolo. Although this was very much 'behind the lines', the move did help to restore a measure of self-respect; for my morale had suffered ever since the day Doreen had been promoted from Driver to Lance-Corporal. A few months after being posted to Isiolo, I was instructed to take over Marsabit District, in the Northern Frontier, charged amongst other things with the task of preparing its evacuation in the face of what at the time seemed an inevitable drive southwards into Kenya from Ethiopia by the Italians. They had long since taken over our stations at Mandera and Moyale; and they controlled the frontier water wells from Lake Rudolf eastwards to the Italian Somaliland border. Wajir and Marsabit we still held, with the former being seriously threatened. All the territory to the north of these stations was a no-man's-land in which the fortunes of war fluctuated with the success or failure of our various 'patrol activities'. Although we usually held our own in these skirmishes, we had no illusions about our ability to withstand any major onslaught; for there was, in fact, nothing capable of holding up an Italian force of even moderate size for more than a few days on their way down to South Africa had they so wished to do that. On paper, the Italians were more than capable of doing this and at the time it was a reasonable assumption that this would happen. Like Mussolini himself, we over-estimated the practical content of such fiercely aggressive phrases as 'a million Italian bayonets', which had been shouted so loudly and for so long. Not that he was at all short of these somewhat outmoded weapons and we were – very.

(2)

After a few months in Isiolo, at that time a hot dustbowl and probably the most unpleasant of all Kenya stations in which to live, the day arrived when I was to set off for Marsabit. I took a minimum of personal property with me. We arranged that Doreen, who had been with me on a few weeks' sick leave, would drive our car down to Nairobi, sell it there for whatever she could get and then continue by train to Mombasa to rejoin her unit at Fortress headquarters. We had become much attached to this old Chevrolet and could not bear the thought of it becoming the property of an Italian officer – even a very senior one – in Marsabit. We had acquired it in Mombasa, just after we had been married, for £90. It let us down almost at once and thereafter more frequently than any other car we have had since. However, it was the only substantial piece of property we owned and was very dear to us. As a parting shot, it broke down before Doreen had completed the first fifty miles to Nanyuki and again between Nanyuki and Nairobi. She touted the car round all the Nairobi garages where all the knowledgeable mechanics shook their heads and said that with the coming petrol shortages there would be no sale for large second-hand cars until the War was over. Their best offer was £10. A woman to whom Doreen had given a lift offered her £50 and, quite rightly, she immediately accepted. We both thought we had been very fortunate to get such a good price. Only a few months later, any vehicle that had four wheels, an engine under the bonnet and a sound petrol tank was worth its weight in gold. The woman buyer had friends in the Army Service Corps and they reconditioned the car for her; soon after it changed hands again at over £300. Anyhow, we had completely avoided the risk of it playing any part in a Roman holiday.

I took a lift to Marsabit with Harry Benson, an Australian stockman engaged in buying cattle for army rations, of whom in due course I was to see much more. One of his affectionate nicknames was 'Silent Harry'. I expect he had trained his voice to carry to all corners of his vast property in Australia, although he himself blamed his inability to reduce its volume to an ordinary level on the fact that he had been brought up shouting at a deaf father.

I must admit that I was very pleased with my new appointment. Not only was the job one that I felt to be more in keeping with the times but it was my first independent command. When you are twenty-seven years old and given charge of an area of 26,000 square miles, you can be forgiven for feeling a little bit inflated and self-satisfied. The fact that these 26,000 square miles contained next to nothing, that over one-third of the area was already more or less in enemy hands and that the whole of it might be any time soon, was quite beside the point.

Once again, I found myself taking over from Jack Wolff but the wind-swept, one-roomed shack, standing on its rocky knoll at Lokitaung, could have been in another world. So was the War. We sat together on a green lawn which fell away in a gentle slope

THE GLITTERING LAKE

in front of a most attractive, whitewashed, thatched cottage. This was the house of the District Commissioner, Marsabit: my home for the next three years. We sipped tea and watched the brightly coloured butterflies fluttering out of the great wall of forest which lay behind us. It was difficult at that moment to believe in anything which was not peaceful; and as we shivered a little in the cool evening air, in spite of the wool pullovers we were wearing, it was certainly very difficult to accept that, just out of our sight, at the foot of the Mountain, a dusty, hot, larva-strewn desert stretched to the horizon in all directions.

Next morning, I awoke at about 7.30 a.m. to my first experience of a damp, solid Marsabit mist and to the sound of an Italian Savoia bomber circling, blind, above it. After Isiolo, it was a lovely, cosy feeling to be able to snuggle down under three blankets. A few weeks previously, the Marsabit airfield had been bombed for the first and as it subsequently turned out, only time. During the following months, Savoia or Capronis bomber aircraft frequently circled the mountain in the early mornings, perhaps just to show some safe, and mild, form of aggression, or maybe really hoping that one day they would find it clear of the thick mist that invariably wrapped the mountain in its damp shroud at that time of the day. At this time, the District Commissioner's house for some reason was relegated to an official no-man's-land, with the main defensive lines (such as they were) located to the rear of it. This provided an even more cosy feeling as I pulled the blankets well up over my chin, watching with one eye the mist swirling in through the open window and listening to the angry drone of the lone aircraft circling high above, wondering if today was the day when it would unleash its bomb load; for the real soldiers stationed at Marsabit had been standing-to in the dripping, sodden forest since an hour before dawn. It made one grateful for being a civilian.

I say 'real soldiers' because a device was employed whereby the minimum disruption of the civil administration was necessary in those parts of Turkana and the Northern Frontier District which had become actual or potential theatres of war.

Like so many brilliant ideas, it was almost childishly simple, although it had met with strong opposition from top army brass when it was put forward. The Officer-in-Charge, Northern Frontier District, a man by the name of Gerald Reece (known to us all, behind his back as 'Uncle'), pushed it through with single-minded determination. He was adamant that the people of the area should not once again be subjected to the upheavals and disasters that had resulted from a ringing of the changes between civil and military government in the early decades of the 20th Century.

The device was merely this: that all administrative officers would be given honorary military rank and carry on the civil government with such minimum modification as circumstances dictated. This was different from what was considered more normal practice, namely that they should be recruited into the Army and given back their jobs as Political Officers, under Army command. The Army naturally thought the idea stupid and quite unworkable. It argued that such a system would render more difficult their task of fighting and winning the war. The higher civil authorities just thought it was probably unworkable. Eventually and sensibly it was decided to try it; Gerald Reece became an honorary Lieutenant-Colonel, his District Commissioners became Honorary Captains and the couple of District officers became Honorary 2nd Lieutenants.

Our instructions were fairly vague: to give all possible assistance to the Army, to remember that there was a war taking place which was important to win, to pay due respect to senior rank and to refrain from our usual practice of wearing a singlet and shorts (or in the case of cold, misty Marsabit, a jersey and corduroy trousers) when on duty. The whole matter was completed with the issue of identity cards confirming we held honorary commissions in the East African Armed Forces and a set of the appropriate number of 'pips' to display on our tunics.

It is true to say that, on paper, an impossible set-up had been created. However, in practice the system worked very well. On-the-whole, I think we all gave reasonable satisfaction to our military superiors 'by consent', while at the same time being able to perform our duties as purely civil administrators. When, before long, our forces penetrated Italian territory instead of the expected vice-versa, modification of the system was very simple. When we crossed the Kenya Frontier into Ethiopia, we automatically became bone-fide Political Officers under direct Army command. In this manner, the early establishment of a rudimentary administration was possible in those areas of occupied enemy territory immediately opposite to us, these areas being regarded as just ad hoc and temporary additions to our existing Kenya districts.

This new system gave us several advantages. We were able to design our own uniforms, shop at the NAAFI and draw army rations on repayment terms when our civilian supplies ran short (and occasionally even a bottle of whiskey). Most importantly, we were now ideally positioned for getting things done the way we thought best and avoiding being mucked about by the Army senior command who, although well intentioned, had not the experience of administrating such areas. To a new Brigadier (or even that rarer of army birds in our area, a Major-General) whom we thought was definitely on the point of wrecking everything, our approach would be:

"Yes, sir. Indeed, I quite understand, sir. However, I'm afraid that is entirely a matter for the civil authorities, sir but I'll most certainly see if we can arrange it so as to meet your wishes, sir."

To the Officer-in-Charge, Northern Frontier District, it would be:

"I'm very sorry, sir but the Brigadier was so upset that I had to change the whole thing. Anyhow, I'm glad to say the result was all right and we were able to get it done without any serious repercussions."

After a while, I even became used to saluting which for some unknown reason I had had a problem with since I had joined the Colonial Service. So much so, that when the late Sir Joseph Byrne, then Governor of Kenya, had paid a visit to the Kitui

District shortly after my arrival and I had dressed in my Field Dress uniform for the first time, I kept my helmet tucked firmly under my arm. When called up to be presented to the Governor, instead of saluting him as etiquette required, I bowed to him gravely. He took this breach of regulations well enough and then noticing something wrong, he stared hard at me:

"Why don't you put your hat on, young man? Dash it all, you'll end up with sunstroke!" He continued to stare.

"Oh – yes; yes, of course, sir, my hat – yes," I mumbled, confused and embarrassed. I took it from under my arm and looked at it with surprise, as if I had never seen the helmet before. I gingerly put it on and eased my way out of the Governor's presence – without saluting.

"What's wrong with that young man? He seems all of a dither," was the only snippet I caught of the ensuing conversation.

In Lodwar, we had a station employee whose mouth was split at each corner, giving him the effect of a permanent grin. Thinking he must have been slashed on the mouth with a knife, I asked him how he had obtained these injuries.

"It was like this," he said. "Just before I was born, my mother went down to the Lake to draw water. As she stooped down, a crocodile came to the surface in front of her, stopped and gave the most stupendous yawn my mother had ever seen. She laughed."

I cannot think what my poor mother did when she was carrying me.

(3)

A string of waterholes was spread along the Marsabit frontier from the eastern tip of Lake Rudolf, at distances varying from five to twenty-five miles apart into Kenya territory – Bani, Buluk, Karsa Bis, El Dimtu, El Yibo, Dukana, El Had, Turbi. On the outbreak of war, these were quickly occupied or came under the control of the Italian forces; Dukana had been the only waterhole where we had normally maintained a small permanent police post. Further south, at distances ranging from fifty to one hundred miles from the frontier was a second string, running south-eastwards from Alia Bay – Karsa, Derati, Galass, Hurran Hurra, North Horr, Kalacha, Gamra, Maikona, Maidahad, Koronle (the last were located on the north-eastern edge of the Chelbi Desert, where the southern lava plateau ended as abruptly as a loosely-built stone wall) and the wells in the Marsabit foothills. A dry-weather, motorable track joined Marsabit to Karsa near the Lake, a distance of about two hundred miles. East of the Marsabit-Turbi track (which eventually reached Moyale on the frontier), there was no permanent water worth mentioning; indeed, to the north of Marsabit lay a vast area of some 8,000 square miles of extreme aridity, much of which was covered in a sea of loose, black, lava rocks known as the Dida Galgalla (The Plain of Darkness).

When I arrived in Marsabit towards the end of 1940, the army garrison there had recently been increased from Company to Battalion strength, plus various odds-and-ends; and outposts were being maintained on the line of the Marsabit – Karsa road. The tribes were kept to the south of this line, at least in theory, and between it and the northern wells now lay a no-man's-land of some 12,000 square miles. Patrolling this area was the responsibility of the Civil Administration, with forces drawn from the establishment of fifty Kenya Police and twenty-five Tribal Police, operating from Marsabit with camel transport and with no faster communication than a camel's (or a man's) legs. It was work they were accustomed to in peace time and the men did it admirably.

The Battalion stationed at Marsabit was the 6th King's African Rifles; the odds-and-ends accompanying it were interesting. The Italians were being active enough in the eastern NFD and the comparative lull on our front gave ample scope for inter-unit squabbles. Compared to what Generals, Admirals and Air Marshals could do (according to their various autobiographies), the display was rather pathetic; but it showed that the artistic temperament develops well below the rank of Lieutenant-Colonel and its equivalents. It was also interesting to observe that even in time of war, a District Commissioner was unable to rid himself of his role of Universal Provider of Comfort for the Mentally Distraught and Recipient of Every Imaginable Tale of Woe ("I feel I shouldn't be worrying you with this but I just don't know who else I can tell." I suppose it still goes on, although judging from the army of experts some DC's have acquired these days, they may now be able to pass the unfortunate person to the District Psychiatrist).

The typical East African European male, whether an official, a farmer or commercial agent was very much an individualist. On the outbreak of war, it was his ambition to be absorbed into some outfit that would provide plenty of scope for that individuality. This would include a maximum of action with a minimum of routine, military discipline. The competition for entry into any formation even slightly irregular was intense; and, as it turned out, a fair choice was provided. We had, for example, at Marsabit regular Irregulars and irregular Irregulars; also, the Kenya Independent Squadron, which was just very irregular. The regular Irregulars were represented by the 2nd Ethiopian Irregulars, one of several units raised from the refugees I have previously mentioned who had entered Kenya through Lokitaung in large numbers towards the end of the Italian-Ethiopian War. They were commanded by Sandy Curle of the Tanganyika Administration. The irregular Irregulars (or 'Bonham's Shifta') were a heterogeneous collection of more recent arrivals who had been enticed across the border by Jack Bonham, of the Kenya Game Department. This outfit was bursting at the seams with irregularity. Jack had made his headquarters in the forest near my house and he shunted his men to and fro to maintain contact with their compatriots in Ethiopia, to take in weapons and to bring back information on the Italian forces' movements. On one occasion, he organised a sizeable airdrop of captured Italian rifles and ammunition.

Needles to say, both Irregular Commanders claimed prior right to provide expert advice on the trans-frontier situation and on Ethiopian affairs in general. Jack Bonham certainly had more immediate and up-to-date contact with the areas right in front of us; but Sandy Curle had access to a more educated and intelligent clientele. He could also claim a trump card in that he had one of the Ethiopian Emperor's cooks in his kitchen. The tide of favour with the local O.C Troops flowed and ebbed erratically and with a maximum of ill-feeling.

The Kenya Independent Squadron (KIS) was formed by Colonel Drought who had raised Drought's Scouts during the First World War. His men were mounted on mules, the majority of which I had been detailed to buy for them from uncooperative Somali owners in Isiolo. The K.I.S. was one of those good ideas in theory but which turns out to have little value in practice. The unit was disbanded not long after it was formed. A rump of optimists was allowed to hang on for a while, as a unit, and remained in Marsabit where they were given the task of watching the north-eastern flank. The unit's commander was an ex-cavalry Captain whose enthusiasm no one could quell but which was based on a military ideology which had faded out round the time of the Siege of Lucknow. He took great pride in the fact that his small unit ("The smallest in the British Army, old boy") was directly facing the enemy. However, his troopers thought that the intervening one hundred miles of waterless desert robbed their task of some of its hazard and romance. Even when the gallant Captain strode at dawn to the forest's edge and flourished his sabre in the general direction of Moyale with a cry of "Behold, the enemy!" his handful of troopers still looked no less browned-off than their mules.

For air support, we had elements of a South African Air Force Co-operation Squadron, flying Hartebeeste biplanes. The men were a fine set of carefree pirates whose sole ambition was to keep flying, non-stop or so it seemed to me. Their private grudge was that they took grave exception to the officers of the K.A.R. The airmen threatened that they would fly no more sorties across the border into Ethiopia until they received at least some friendly overtures from what they alleged were the surly, stiff-necked, tight-lipped, red tape-bound Englishmen. They continued making these sorts of utterances for some time but, in practice, they and the officers of the K.A.R. seemed to rub along quite well. They certainly never took any active steps which might reduce their flying time. On one occasion, they averted a crisis by volunteering to bring up from Nairobi a large consignment of silver shillings to buy cattle for the army rations; at that time, no tribesman, quite understandably, would accept paper money. Nothing much seemed to be happening and a few days later, I went down to their camp in the forest, about a mile or so from my office. I was in a most anxious state of mind. I reached the campsite to find it, to my great surprise, completely deserted. There was not soul in sight. It seemed that the S.A.A.F. had decamped the previous day on some other urgent re-posting. No-one had bothered to inform me. On searching around, I discovered the cash boxes, containing the equivalent of some £2000, dumped but still intact, beneath the trees.

In time, I became used to the fact that no-one seemed to tell me anything apart from their private troubles and what was needed to be done to win the war in six months. Even the daily password often missed me out and this was often a trying affair. Sentries have always scared me and at this time they were all so trigger-happy that it could be quite harrowing. The picture-book sort of sentry was not so bad. He stood in the centre of the road with his fixed bayonet pointed menacingly at your navel and fiercely barked the Swahili equivalent of "Halt, who goes there?" Sometimes, if you were quick off the mark and asked him what today's password was, he would tell you, equally fiercely. You then repeated it formally to him and he would relax, go through all the motions and end with a rifle butt salute which rang through the forest. It was the nasty, informal type of sentry who tended to materialise suddenly from nowhere, with camouflage grass and leaves in his hat, that really got me down. This was particularly true of the ones who took a poor view of being asked the password instead of being given it.

(4)

Some months passed in an atmosphere of semi-phoney war, relieved by the inevitable 'patrol activity'. The 2nd Irregulars were withdrawn from their lakeside post at Karsa. The Gelubba, now reinforced with Italian rifles to replace their ancient 'Fusil Gras', took the opportunity to have a few swipes at the Gabbra. The K.A.R. mounted an attack on Italian-occupied Dukana and pushed out the Banda. They then withdrew and handed it over temporarily to the 2nd Irregulars. At that time, I was on safari in the North Horr area and spent the first night of their occupation with them. The Irregulars were very much at home in the bush and had improvised impressive defences around the small stone-walled fort. Their officers included a Kenya civil servant, a naturalised Austrian white hunter and a Polish ex-night club proprietor from Addis Ababa, the capital of Ethiopia. I regret to say that even here some ill-feeling was poured out on the District Commissioner's breast: why should the Irregulars have to do all the dirty work while the flat-footed K.A.R. went back to Marsabit, home and beauty? Although a counterattack from the El Yibo wells was expected, the night passed quietly in our blacked-out, fortified encampment.

This was a period of depression, of rumours of total withdrawal. Petty animosities were rife, set aside only in the expression of a general longing to do something positive. Tribal morale was also low. There were indications that both the Gabbra and the Boran, whose ancestral homes were in southern Ethiopia, where the greater part of the tribes still lived, were becoming more pro-Italian, backing them as the most likely victors. Meanwhile, business was brisk in the selling of information to both sides by professional intelligence agents. Rumours of alleged lack of initiative on the part of some of our troops, many of whom were by now becoming bored with the whole affair, spread from waterhole to waterhole. It became more and more difficult to purchase the full quota of cattle and goats required as army rations, even at enhanced prices. Although we had a warning to expect continuous air raids, nothing happened, except that one afternoon a lone Capri flew over my office and fired off a few rounds as it crossed the landing-strip further down the hill.

Very simple actions sometimes have surprisingly far-reaching results. When the war began, the flagpole, which stood in the centre of the grass lawn in front of the tiny, thatched, District Office building, was removed. The theory was that this would render the district headquarters less identifiable from the air by the Italian bombers. In fact, with or without the flagpole, the station with its lawns, paths and symmetrical Police lines stood out from the air as clearly as anything could stand out. The flagpole not having been in place when I arrived in Marsabit, I had never really thought about it. However, in attempting to evolve something to raise tribal morale, I consciously noticed its absence one morning as I sat at my desk gazing through the open doorway of the office building at the green lawns and the forest wall beyond. At once, I got up from my chair and went in search of the pole. We found it in a storeroom, buried beneath some old sacks and pieces of timber. We laid it on the ground outside and, after a thorough dusting-down, we gave it a new coat of white paint. It was a magnificent pole, tall and almost straight, having many years before been carefully selected from the forest. You might say that it was the pride of the Northern Frontier District as far as flagpoles were concerned. We spent most of the next day struggling to erect it in place on the lawn in front of the District headquarters. I arranged a short but emotional ceremony with a parade of smartly dressed Kenya and Tribal Police combined with a few army personnel. The whole parade saluted as the Union Jack was slowly hauled up the flag post. The effect of this exercise was so immediate that I wished I had had the sense to think of it sooner. The word spread rapidly from one end of the District to the other, in essence: "The D.C.'s flag is up again, the British must be going to win the war!" Tribal spirits brightened noticeably and had no time to fall by the time the first group of South African Majors arrived.

(5)

I do not think anyone bothered to tell me officially that the white population of my district was about to be increased from a mere handful to over nine thousand. The first real inkling I got of it was the appearance of the Majors. This was a rank with which I became very familiar. Just as the lowest visible commissioned rank in the United States Air Force is undoubtedly Lieutenant-Colonel, the South African forces seemed to have made a corner in Majors. It was not until many years later, when I was posted to St Lucia, in the West Indies, that I learned about the Lieutenant-Colonels, so I was very prepared to be impressed by the lower rank when it first invaded Marsabit. The Majors usually turned up in groups of three to six and at odd hours of the day and night. Like their more elevated American allies, they were inclined to be thirsty on arrival and to carry very bulky briefcases.

Be that as it may, we were all very pleased to see the first wave of Majors. Of course, they were unable to tell us very much because secrecy is vital to the successful prosecution of war. However, when a request is made for preparation of miles of camping sites, millions of gallons of water and hundreds of head of cattle, you can but draw your own conclusions. The immediate result of the Majors' hush-hush visit was most impressive. It really put the District back on its feet again, ready to win any war anywhere and to hell with Mussolini. This was the arrival of a section of armoured cars – and were we pleased to see them! That some of this vintage subsequently turned out not to be bullet-proof was neither here nor there. Now indeed, we had a tangible sign of the Empire's might and, following hard on the heels of the D.C.'s flag-raising, all tribal waverers were put to shame. The Swahili word for both 'rhino' and 'armoured fighting vehicle' is 'kifaru' (plural 'vifaru') and the arrival of these vifaru spread as swiftly as bushfire through an Australian gum tree forest. A quick flame of rumour roared quickly over the heads of the population to the effect that a hundred vifaru had arrived; this was followed by the slow-moving, fiery wall of more consolidated rumour which put the figure at nine hundred and fifty-two (preciseness being the essence of a genuine rumour).

The succeeding steps in the South African occupation of Marsabit are a blurred memory of utter chaos. The 2nd Brigade was followed by 1st Division headquarters and the 5th Brigade; battalions of the Transvaal Scottish, the South African Irish, the Regiment Botha and the 1st and 2nd Field Force Battalions all rolled into the forest glades in a crescendo of dust and noise. Roads which were not much more than tracks scraped on the laval rock and dust and which had carried a couple of trucks a week adequately, now disintegrated completely when required to carry thousands. Field Artillery and Heavy Workshops finally demolished them, although it was not long before the magnificent South African Road Construction Companies gave us back the finest dirt roads in Kenya. In addition to Anti-Aircraft units and everything else which goes to make up a Divisional centre, we had several squadrons of motor cyclists. Next to the ill-fated muleteers of the Kenya Independent Squadron, these must have been the most disappointed and frustrated soldiers of the war. They had, I gathered, been brought up in the best cavalry traditions; while it may be too much to say that they literally imagined themselves going into action with screaming, kilted infantrymen clinging to their foot-rests, they certainly were confident that the day would come when they would charge in line abreast, engines roaring, upon the enemy. The enemy, of course, would be completely terrorised by the blast of the sirens which were fitted to each machine for this very purpose. The motor cyclists looked with pleasurable anticipation at the glorious flatness of the Chelbi Desert on their maps. If only the enemy had decided to come down that far and had been foolish enough to march along it in columns of four, these enthusiasts might have been able to fulfil their hopes and dreams. As it was, they floundered about on their motor bikes in the deep, powdered lava dust with both feet on the ground, for all the world like rudderless boats in a heavy sea, both men and engines coughing and spluttering in a desperate and generally unsuccessful attempt to remain mobile.

(6)

Although I had not been in Marsabit for long by the time the South African invasion took place, I should by then have known all there was to know about the forest streams and watering places, for they were few enough in number. In mitigation, I had no forewarning that such an event was about to take place. A Division requires a great deal of water and I was unable to give them all the advice and information they required on how to obtain it. Divisional Headquarters thereupon came up with the idea of turning loose a few hundred men in the forest to scour it for water sources, including the bandsmen.

It is a common fallacy to assume that because a man is a South African (or indeed, an Australian) he is *ipso facto* accustomed to the wide-open spaces and well-versed in bush-craft. More than likely, he will turn out to come from Johannesburg (or Sydney) and to be about as up-to-date in his bush-craft as an average member of the London County Council. When evening came of the day of releasing the men into the forest, a good many of the men were still missing and so search parties were dispatched. The whole situation became farcical. Some of the original lost men then turned up while some of the search parties became lost. A running score was kept and by the time I left Headquarters, the number missing at any given moment varied between about five and twenty-five. Messengers were dashing in and out and the harassed G.S.O.3 had his scoreboard in a frightful mess. Well into the night, there were still a few missing, including several bandsmen. They turned up during the next day, weary, unkempt and hungry but triumphant. Two men of the Regiment Botha had found a magnificent water supply; the name was known to me but I had not known its size (when you ask a Boran about any of these streams or pools the reply always indicates a cross between the Niagara Falls and Kaietor Falls). As far as the South Africans were concerned, they had discovered a brand-new stream, previously completely unknown and that was that. We did not waste time trying to disillusion them: any attempt would have been quite unsuccessful, for we all have a touch of Martin Johnson in our blood. Sometime later, I succeeded in officially re-naming the stream 'Botha Falls', as a permanent reminder of the South African occupation of Marsabit.

Naturally, we were quite apprehensive about the possible repercussions of dropping thousands of white South Africans into what had been an entirely black African district. We also were concerned how they would get on with the Police and Tribal Police who were to supply guide sections for them at all levels. In the end, our worries came to nothing because they all got on in a way which did credit to the good sense of all parties. To see 'armed natives' was a quite shattering experience for most of the white South Africans, for it was something beyond their understanding and the sort of thing they had been brought up to believe was just not possible. To each battalion, we allotted a section of Police and Tribal Police guides, with senior N.C.O.'s as liaison officers at Divisional and Brigade Headquarters. Through their friendliness, smartness, skill and great desire to help, these guides soon became extremely popular with all South African ranks.

To illustrate this, I was sitting one evening with a Brigade Major in his tent when one of our best Police Sergeants (a Kamba from the Machakos District) happened to walk past the entrance. This sergeant was attached to Brigade Headquarters. The major watched him until out of site and he then turned to me and said quietly: "There goes quite the smartest soldier in my Brigade." Indeed, some of these guides became quite spoilt. They were overwhelmed with South African rations and were given gifts of one kind or another, including photographs of

General Smuts. On one occasion, I asked a South African Corporal whom I had come to know rather well, how the men were settling down with the 'armed natives'. He scratched his head, thought for a moment and then said: "It all seemed a bit strange at first and some of the boys didn't like it at all. We had an argument about it in the mess one evening. In the end, one of the men said: 'What I think is that if their Government thinks they're good enough to carry arms and to fight this war with us, then they're good enough for me.' And that's how we look at it now."

Looking back at that time, I can recall only one incident which had anything to do with colour and it was not one of the locals who was concerned. I think our only legitimate grumble was that when a motorised fighting patrol was attacked at Turbi, on the Moyali road, the resulting issue of decorations did not include a young Police guide whose alertness and bravery was reported to have saved the patrol from taking heavy casualties. We managed to have him awarded the East African Force Badge but felt it was not quite the same thing.

We ran a few football teams in Marsabit, made up from the Police, prison warders and others. However, with so many men constantly out on patrol, we were always short. 'Ba' Allen, the Assistant Inspector of Police (the highest police rank Marsabit could boast up to that time), had made a big impression with the South Africans. He persuaded some of the South Africans to fill in the missing positions, including a few of the most dyed-in-the-wool Afrikaaners. They joined our mixed teams with some trepidation but after a game or two became most enthusiastic in their participation. One day, however, none of them turned up for a match. We received an abject apology and an explanation for their absence. It seemed that 'the Predikant' – a Dutch Reformed Church Army Chaplain – was about to arrive and he would be deeply opposed to them playing football with black Africans. They thought he would certainly report the matter back to the South African Union Government and thereby cause such a political issue that they could not risk continuing to behave in such an immoral, albeit enjoyable, way.

The South African occupation was a hectic time for everyone but nonetheless a happy time. The South Africans could hardly have been kinder than they were both to me and to our oddly assorted district staff. They were also considerate towards any tribesmen with whom they came into contact, once they became reconciled to the fact that this God-forsaken country was really these people's home and that we had no intention of 'clearing' it for them. Excellent relations were maintained and I, certainly, had no cause to complain; for although I was only a youngster, Major-General George Brink who commanded the 1st Division, never failed to treat me with a great deal more courtesy than my civilian, let alone my military, rank entitled me. Furthermore, he was always ready to consider and accept my advice on local matters.

On one evening, I was returning with him and a Staff officer to his camp. We were extremely surprised to find a forlorn-looking baby camel tethered close by to the Major-General's tent. He shouted for his batman who came running at the double with a worried expression on his face.

"Joubert, what's the meaning of this? What's this animal?"

"It's – it's – a camel, sir"

"I know it's a camel, idiot but whose is it?"

"It's m-m-mine, sir"

"You mean you have bought it?"

"Yes, sir – for twenty shillings, sir."

"But why? What on earth for, Joubert?"

"For a novelty, sir."

Shortly after the South Africans' arrival, a patrol opened fire with every weapon they had on a harmless party of Rendille moving to another grazing ground (at the Brigade Commander's request). Fortunately, this resulted in only some minor injuries and a couple of dead camels for which full compensation was later paid. Apart from this incident, the only subject on which any real awkwardness arose was in connection with the shooting of wild game animals.

Most South Africans, like most Americans, have a passion for 'hunting'; almost any creature, provided it is alive, is regarded as suitable quarry. It was understandable, to some extent, that when they came to fight a war and found themselves in the great wastes of Marsabit District, they should have felt it their right to shoot without discrimination or restriction. It probably never occurred to most of them that there could be any possible objection to shooting. The Kenya Government, equally naturally, had a quite different idea. Unless the territory had to be surrendered to the enemy, it would continue to preserve the wonderful asset of its wildlife, to whatever extent it possibly could.

The Marsabit elephant, fortunately, took care of themselves: they just cleared off the Mountain as soon as the first army conveys arrived. To this day, I have no idea where they went. It was the best part of two years before we saw them again. They kept well out of the way until they were quite sure that the army had gone for good. The rhino, except for a few who broke their necks charging trucks on the road, and the buffalo, were also more or less able to look after themselves. It was the giraffe, the kudo, the zebra and the commoner kinds of antelope which suffered, although it was only after two major massacres that we really started to put on the screws in which we had the full support of the South African authorities.

The first of these massacres was an organised hunt by a large party of soldiers who surrounded a mixed herd of Grant's Gazelle, Oryx and zebra and opened-up on the animals with rifle and light automatic fire. The results are best left to the imagination. Suffice it to say that hardly an animal survived the slaughter. The second occasion concerned a semi-tame herd of eight giraffe which used to wander round the lower slopes of the mountain on the north-west side. One day, this herd quite without concern browsed up to an outpost on the North Horr road. A Major found this too much for his sporting instincts and promptly shot seven of them, the eighth getting away, although wounded. When with barely disguised anger, I asked why he had shot them, he was most surprised to learn that he had done anything wrong. He gave as his reason (and more-or-less the same one Sir Edmund Hillary gave when asked why men climb mountains) "Well, man – they were there." The seven martyred giraffe did not die in vain, for this incident incensed so many people that the local command threw its full weight into game preservation.

(7)

At the beginning of February 1941, the long-awaited moment came. Orders were given for the South African Army to move out of Marsabit and to push north-west into Ethiopia. The frontier was crossed near Dukana and the Italians were driven first from their garrisons at Hobol, Gorai and El Gumu and then from their main base at Mega. The Chelbi Desert 'road' became more than a mile wide in places as each succeeding convoy made a new track for itself, in an attempt to escape from the deep drifts of powder-fine soda dust. Elsewhere, the broad swathes cleared through the light, friable, lava soils by the bulldozers of the Road Construction companies, quickly became deep rivers of red, choking, all-pervading dust, through which the vehicles bounced and reared, each invisible within its own cloud. The Italians had shown little enterprise when the Division had been encamped on the fringes of the highly combustible, lichen-covered, Marsabit Forest; they showed none at all now.

We fondly thought this was it and the South African troops were all set to fight their way to Addis Abbaba itself; but it soon became apparent that the Division's strategic role was merely to execute a left-hook feint. The South Africans first step into enemy territory was naturally an occasion to be made the most of and special arrangements were made to film and record the event. A spot thought to be right on the frontier boundary

THE GLITTERING LAKE

line was selected. It was probably as good a guess as any, for up to that time the boundary had never been accurately fixed in that area. A notice board was erected which announced in large letters (in English and Afrikaans) 'This was the Frontier'. The G.O.C. in his staff car drove across, preceded and followed by armoured cars. The cameras whirred and the commentator shouted stirring words into his recorder about how this had been the first time the frontier had been crossed by the army. About a mile further on, the party overtook a bulldozer; the driver, stripped to the waist and covered with red dust, was calmly ploughing his lonely road towards the enemy.

I travelled up to Dukana to observe how the Police guides we had provided to the army were getting on. I walked in on the Brigade mess for breakfast, to be met with good-humoured banter to the effect that they really had thought that they had escaped from all stupid, civilian restrictions and were at last to be allowed to fight their war. I lifted a case of canned beer off them and a Major (inevitably) took me on a guided tour of the Hobol and Gorai battlefields. These were miserable places to be fighting for - and the fighting involved dying, as the fresh graves signified. The next day, I drove back to North Horr and from there to Marsabit the following morning. The place seemed dull and very empty. An East African Colonel arrived to take over Lines of Communication command. The party was clearly over and I felt deflated and out of a job.

(8)

In the middle of that February, I received an order requesting me to proceed with all possible speed to 1st South African Division Headquarters and to place myself under the command of the General Officer Commanding, for political duties. I detailed staff to accompany me, packed up my 3-ton International truck with what seemed to be the appropriate kit and made all necessary preparations to leave Marsabit the next morning.

As far as I knew, the Division was still at Kunchurro. With

the appallingly mangled state of the roads, I thought it would probably take me the best part of three days to reach there. As I was sitting down to a rather late lunch, a couple of South African Air Force pilots (one of whom I had known for some time) suddenly appeared from nowhere. When they heard what I was planning to do, they immediately suggested I squeeze into their Hartebeeste biplane, as they were on their way to the Division themselves. After mentally weighing up the pros and cons, of which there were many, and on being assured I could bring with me a camp bed and one small suitcase, I decided to accept their offer. I arranged for the truck's departure the next day, gave the two airmen beds for the night and prepared myself for take-off at noon the next day.

The Hartebeeste had two open cockpits and, as the guest traveller, I was given the gunner's seat in the rear while he stood between my knees in a position where he could just about manoeuvre his machine gun. The cockpit was a tight fit for one; for two, it was, well, just tight. I had been quite proud of myself in improvising personal 'flying kit' in the shape of a beret and a pair of motoring goggles. Both were blown off within the first ten minutes of our flight. Our first task was to drop a message at North Horr and we spiralled down to accomplish this through a typically bumpy desert atmosphere. By this time, I had a very stiff neck and could not summon up much interest in our flight. It was only when we finally circled round the small hills at Kunchurro that I began to take much notice. A harsh gale was sweeping across the rough landing ground which had been bulldozed out of the heavy bush. I breathed a sigh of relief as we descended and made our landing approach. This relief was premature because no sooner had the pilot got the wheels of the lurching aircraft near the ground than he zoomed skywards again. On his third attempt, the aircraft managed to touch down in a very one-point landing. I was un-wedged from my seat, hauled out and pushed and pulled into something resembling normal human shape again. The pilot was most apologetic about it all and remarked that the aircraft had been already slightly overweight before I came aboard.

I now metaphorically removed my District Commissioner's hat and donned that of a Political Officer. I reported to the G.O.C. and was duly instructed to travel to Mega the next day to assist the 5th Brigade in administrative and political matters. Someone gave me the corner of a grubby tent and I spent what remained of the day in gingerly unscrewing my neck and generally recovering from my flight from Marsabit. In the process, I found time to congratulate myself on having accomplished what would have been a very difficult three-day journey in a mere one and a half hours, which seemed to me to be a reasonable interpretation of my orders.

Next morning, I hitched a lift with a couple of ubiquitous Majors. After travelling with some caution, on account of reports that Banda were still operating in the area, we reached Mega at about 4.30 in the afternoon. However, I arrived without my kit, which was frustrating. Another Major, doing his best to be helpful no doubt, had put it on a vehicle travelling in a different convoy. After much searching, I managed to find it in the late evening with some friends in the 22nd East African Pioneers. Mega was at an altitude of about 6000 feet above sea level and the night was very cold. I made up my camp bed beneath a thorn bush. It was with relief that I crawled under my blankets and was able to relax. It had been a hard day and I was thankful it was at an end. The stars of the Milky Way above me were as bright as fireflies in the cold night air. I slept soundly until the rising sun next morning suddenly smacked me in the eye.

(9)

The South Africans were required to do some considerable fighting in the capture of Mega, in difficult terrain made no easier by the onset of the rains. Looking back now, it seems very small stuff in the perspective of great events and final victory; and in the light of the subsequent lightning campaign in which, save towards the end, it was a matter of some difficulty to catch up with the retreating Italians, even on the excellent road system which they had so quickly built through previously roadless Ethiopia. But in February 1941, allied victories were not all that common and in Kenya we had barely become used to the idea that the Italians were not going to invade the country after all. The South Africans had felt that they really had not come all this way north to sit about in the Kenya deserts; and the rest of us had become tired of being depressed and of expecting to beat an ignominious retreat at any moment. Occupied Mega was a cheerful place, morale was high and everyone was in good spirits, even the Political officer. That optimistic mood of mine lasted for two days. The Army had done what it had come to do and for those first two days I, also, was one of those conquering heroes. On the third day, it began to dawn on me the enormous mess I was supposed to sort out.

I established myself in the Round House, which had been the home of the Italian Residente and a prominent feature of Mega. Modelled on an Ethiopian 'tukal', or rondavel-type house, it had a single room in the middle, a circular passage around this, and other rooms on the outside of the passage, both offices and living quarters. The greater part of the central room was a beautifully fitted-up bathroom and lavatory – extremely high-class and very different from the little house around the corner which was all we ran to in Marsabit - and in most other Kenya out-stations. The snag, very soon discovered, was that all this ultra modernity ended with the chromium and tiles; the more essential if less aesthetic features, namely, the drains, were just non-existent.

I cajoled the Brigadier into allocating me one of three small, civilian cars which had been captured, but as competition was very keen, I lost this to some higher dignitary after a few days. This car had been acquired in what we all agreed had been an essentially unsporting way. It had been driven into our lines in all innocence by an Italian officer from Neghelli, a town to the north, the morning after Mega had fallen to the South Africans. He had been coming to spend a few days with the Residente and had just happened to be out of touch with the latest local news.

On the 26th February, we had a ceremonial parade on the square in front of the Round House to mark the capture of Mega. The Brigadier took a salute and inspected a Guard of Honour mounted by the Transvaal Scottish, who then marched past in review order to the skirl of their pipes. A brass band played selections of martial music and I was detailed to read 'Proclamation No. 1 – Enemy Occupied Territory Administration' – duly interpreted clause by clause into Amharic and Boran. I doubt if this made it any more intelligible to the gaping populace who were, in any case, very much more interested in and impressed by the bands. Then we had some official photographs taken, with the usual confusion about the twining of knees to the left or the right. It was all quite rousing in its way and we wondered how we had ever felt it might be difficult to win the war. The ladies of the village (with the very best intentions, for one could hardly expect them to appreciate such niceties as the difference between the Italian and the South African outlook) put on their best finery and streamed up the hill in most colourful procession to Brigade HQ to place their services jointly and severally at the victors disposal. Their reception was cold. They hung around for some time muttering disbelief and disappointment, with an occasional little shriek as the enormity of the present and the bleakness of the future situation slowly dawned on the intelligentsia. They were shoed away and they straggled down to the town in dejected little groups, sadder, if not better, women. It was a sight which would have cheered the heart of the Predikant, had he been there to witness it.

The 2nd South African Brigade had been deployed to recapture the main Kenya frontier station of Moyale, which had been in Italian hands almost since the entry of Italy into the war but, in the event, they were forestalled by detachments of the 2nd Irregulars who, with great glee, got in before them. Moyale had considerable prestige value; with the tribes astride the frontier, its re-occupation greatly advanced the British cause, just as its erstwhile capture by the Italians had put them temporarily in the local ascendancy. The Italians had made much propaganda out of its capture and now we did the same. In fact, Moyale had had a rather chequered war-time history. It had always been assumed in Kenya that Italy would enter a war simultaneously with Germany and no one foresaw the time lag. On the declaration of war with Germany, a telegram received in Moyale was interpreted to mean that Italy was also an enemy. The station was evacuated, only to be hastily and blushingly, re-occupied. The mistake was, however, quite popular with the local tribes on both sides of the border, as they had just enough time to fit in a masterly looting operation.

I travelled to Moyale and was asked by the Brigadier to make various political and administrative arrangements with what he referred to as the 'Sultans and Chieftains'. These had come in to Moyale to declare unswerving loyalty to what now looked like the winning side. However, it soon became apparent that these men were a collection of riff-raff and Teddy Boys from the township; but some of the real tribal authorities eventually did turn up. Gerald Reece (who became the Senior Political Officer as soon as he had one foot across the frontier) arrived to take part in the ceremonial re-establishment of the lawful Kenya frontier. I shared a too-hastily erected tent with him and it collapsed on us during a heavy thunderstorm in the middle of the night. Even this did not dampen our rejoicing at seeing the 'Union Jack' once more flying from the crumbling, mud tower of Fort Rose. Although this fort was no longer of any military value, it was one of our few treasured 'ancient monuments' in the Northern Frontier District. Gerald Reece had been District Commissioner, Moyale, for a long period previous to the war. Although it quite embarrassed him when, every now and then, some long-lost friend would dash out of the crowd and fling himself on the ground to kiss his feet, these and other spontaneous gestures of relief and friendship certainly gave the impression that some other people shared our views.

(10)

The hasty retreat of the Italians following the capture of Mega and Moyale left an area of some 15,000 square miles, from the Omo River eastwards, in a state of complete lawlessness where no writ ran. It was rugged country with scarcely a motorable track and it was in complete chaos. Many Italian levies and some regular troops had just returned to their homes, taking their weapons with them; others had formed themselves into gangs of bandits. Most of the tribesmen to whom arms had hastily been given in the hope that they would use them against the British advance, realised they could put the weapons to much better use in paying off old scores. It is difficult for anyone accustomed to civilised government to imagine what can happen when it ceases to exist even in its most elementary form. At Mega, it was made very clear how much even those of us who have lived in some quite lawless places take for granted. Some years later, the then Governor of Kenya was telling me about a conversation he had just had with the current and very important visiting Member of Parliament. He ended by saying, with a deep sigh: "His views are sound enough and he means very well but the trouble with these chaps and anyone else whose life is saturated with the British background and nothing else, is that they can never conceive of a situation arising in which someone might open up on them with a sub-machine gun as they walk down the garden path to catch the 9.30 to Westminster."

In theory we were, along with the rest of the allied world, rejoicing that all these people had been freed from the Italian yoke. However, the liberated inhabitants of this extensive no-man's-land between the armies were chiefly engaged in mutual looting, murder and massacre. Anyone temporarily on the receiving end and within reach of Mega, hastily sent in envoys begging protection and punitive measures against their enemies. There was very little we could do about this situation for the time being. There were certainly times when it was heartbreaking not to be able to provide help even in the face of the most desperate and genuine need. Very quickly our little victories, of which we had been so proud, lost their glamour in the context of the subsequent human suffering occurring all round us.

Detachments of Ethiopian Irregulars and East African Pioneers were eventually put at my disposal as 'police'. A regular system of patrols into the surrounding countryside was instigated. By this means, some form of order, if little law, was gradually established, although it was not the sort of work for which these units had been either raised or trained. When one takes into consideration the general chaos and the improvised arrangements established to cope with it, unfortunate incidents were few. I do not think it had ever occurred to anyone that the Italians would vanish over the horizon as rapidly as they did.

One evening, a white-faced and strained-looking young British Sergeant, who had come straight from Britain to a posting with one of these units, reported back from a patrol, of which he had been in charge. Holding back a lot of emotion, he reported to me that he had successfully cleared up the various murders and other crimes he had been dispatched to investigate. However, "he didn't think he was cut out to be a policeman", and he hoped he would not be given such a job again. It turned out that his methods had been direct and simple. He had called together the elders of the villages which had suffered and asked them who was mainly responsible for certain crimes. A particular man was identified as the ringleader and the sergeant took him around the corner and shot him with his revolver. The second-in-command of the patrol was an Ethiopian who had given him categorical assurances that this was the normal and accepted way of dealing with such criminals.

(11)

Shortly after the capture of Mega, the Italians evacuated Yavello, a small town some sixty miles to the north. By this time, the South Africans had been pulled out and their place had been taken by the East African Infantry Brigade. This Brigade received orders that Yavello was to be formally occupied. As operations in the country were now in aid of restoration of the Emperor of Ethiopia's Government, a high Ethiopian official, Dedesmatch Abeba Dimtu, was brought in to accompany the army column so that he could take over the town in the Emperor's name.

The column consisted of a Company of the 4th K.A.R., a few armoured cars and various hangers-on like me. Things were quite impressive until the armoured cars became bogged down in the first patches of black cotton soil we encountered, from which they were eventually, if ingloriously, pulled out by a civilian vehicle. This vehicle, inevitably, belonged to Harry Benson, the stockman, who with true Australian perspicacity and determination, succeeded in becoming involved in any show that happened to be on the road. Cattle, after all, were ubiquitous and could always be investigated if not actually bought. (I myself had, in fact, no very valid reason for being present). We had been warned that there was a minefield on the outskirts of Yavello but the column went through it without mishap. We removed sixteen mines, missing a few which subsequently damaged heavier artillery transport the next day.

Having safely negotiated the minefield, we reformed for the triumphal procession into Yavello. White flags fluttered from many of the houses and the road was thinly lined with people waving them. The most popular model of flag had been quickly improvised from strips of looted toilet paper. Occasionally, the column was held up by someone dashing on to the road and throwing himself down to kiss the ground in front of the Dedesmatch's car. One such enthusiast narrowly missed having to be scraped off a wheel.

Before our arrival, Yavello had been occupied by Patriots. Their patriotism, in addition to cleaning out the town, had extended to committing several very unpleasant murders and the collection of 'taxes' from all and sundry. Many of the townspeople were members of the Burji, Konzo and kindred 'slave tribes' and this section of the community showed little enthusiasm for the return of their Amharic overlords. We had been in the town for only a few hours when I received a deputation requesting the British to stay away, please. The answer was simple but my attempts to paint a picture of a glorious, new, free and democratic Ethiopia fell a bit flat. One of our incidental objectives had been to rescue from a nearby Catholic Mission two Italian priests who had managed so far to avoid being mopped up in the general outburst of patriotism. Among the very few possessions they were able to carry away with them was a bottle of Aquavite. A few weeks later this bottle formed the basis of a farewell party they held for some of us, on the eve of their departure for an internment camp.

During the first night of our stay in Yavello, a single light-machine gun opened fire on the town from the nearby hills. Along with a motley collection of camp-followers in the shape of Intelligence, Revolt, Counter-revolt, Supply and irregular Irregulars, I had commandeered the least uncomfortable-looking empty house I could find and we were all very upset that the realities of war should so rudely disturb what had looked like being the makings of a first class party. Its beginnings had, in fact, already been interrupted by Counter-Intelligence, who, being one of those unfortunate men who become surprisingly drunk on very little, had wandered out into the streets. He was shot at by sentries, fought with those who attempted to rescue him and ended up under extremely close and very noisy, arrest. This episode made those of us in the 'hangers-on' contingent somewhat unpopular and with dawn also came the first of a series of very justifiable dirty looks.

Two days later, I took a lift in Revolt's staff car back to Mega. Ambushes had been prophesied but the journey was quite uneventful. The careful attention I had paid to instructions on how to fire a tommy-gun through a windscreen with minimum damage to me, had all been wasted. After the completion of various conferences, I handed over the Round House and my administrative job to Gordon Skipper, a tough and energetic man from New Zealand. He had an ability to get things done and done quickly, which I had always envied. He had developed considerable local fame for his handling of a very tiresome V.I.P. at Wajir. This man had ended a trying afternoon by asking "Isn't there anything else you can show me, Skipper? There must be some interesting things round here." To which Gordon replied: "Yes sir, actually there is – there's a dead camel just outside the village. Would you care to see that?"

On the trip back to Marsabit, I was accompanied by Ba Allen who had arrived in Mega from the Lake to report that the Gelubba were showing no signs of activity. It proved to be the last time for several years that any such statement could be made; and it was not strictly true even when it was made.

Our two trucks were heavily laden and it took three full, arduous days to grind and bump our way back to Marsabit. At Kunchurro, we learned that two days previously a Gelubba raiding party had attacked a Boran encampment nearby, killing eleven people. As a result of this raid, the remaining Boran had scattered into the bush. We travelled through completely deserted countryside until we reached North Horr. The journey had a dreamlike quality as we lumbered along the appalling track, picking our way through the scattered debris of an army. We wished that we had access to another truck in which we could load the more useful items, so many of which would be extremely welcome now that we had to face a relapse into a state of semi-civilian impoverishment.

This turned out to be our last trip to or from Mega in such discomfort, for a magnificent new road, through the Hurri Hills and up the Mega escarpment, was nearing completion. So was a telephone line from Isiolo to Marsabit which had been originally planned to simplify communications between Nairobi and Headquarters, 1st South African Division. The bare poles meandered into the silent forest, the last one standing sentinel over the remains of General Brink's camp. Had the pole borne arms, they would surely have been reversed. The poles looked lonely and forlorn, perhaps slightly disappointed that they had played no part in the war which had now passed them by. Some three months later, the wires were added; I now had the unprecedented luxury of a telephone in my office. Somewhat to my surprise, the system even worked, when giraffe and Rendille youths, who valued the copper wire, permitted. The young Rendille men had also discovered with delight that the large nuts on the wire strainers made club heads of exceptional efficiency when correctly embedded in a local glue. The giraffe had their own amusements with the leaning poles and sagging wires which resulted.

CHAPTER SEVEN

AFTERMATH

(1)

With the sudden disappearance of the War to the far north, the Marsabit District became very much 'lines of communication', although Brigade Headquarters, with responsibilities on both sides of the Lake, was maintained there until February 1942. The immediate situation as regards frontier security was serious. Such troops as were available had static roles to play and our Kenya Police and Tribal Police were decimated on account of the numbers still scattered about on duty with various military units. In the delta Lake area, the Gelubba were receiving substantial reinforcement from both abandoned Italian weaponry and the willing services of various wandering ex-soldiers from both their regular and irregular forces. In addition, several well-organised bands of brigands were operating elsewhere along the frontier.

The Gelubba wasted little time and were soon raiding deep into the district; indeed, on one occasion, raiding right into the foothills of Marsabit Mountain. By the end of May 1941, Gabbra casualties (mostly women and children) had passed the sixty mark and their stock losses were heavy. There were rumours, not perhaps so far-fetched, of a major Gelubba invasion. With one thing and another, our change over from an operational to a non-operational area substantially increased the hazards to life and property for the civilian population. If the security situation worsened, comparatively large numbers of troops would have had to be deployed in the area and so withdrawn from the on-going war effort to the north. The only practical way of dealing with the situation was to mount an expedition from both sides of the Lake to clean out the delta area with one, swift blow. The Brigadier strongly supported this proposal, and plans were drawn up along the lines of a classic pincer movement. A battalion of King's African Rifles, supported by some five hundred armed Gabbra and Rendille levies would move into the delta area up the east shore of the Lake while a somewhat smaller regular force, supported by a thousand Turkana levies, would push simultaneously in from the west.

I set about the task of raising a suitable force of levies, for which masses of captured Italian rifles were available. I also organised the animal transport required for our part of the expedition, estimated at three hundred camels. Needless-to-say, local tribal enthusiasm knew no bounds, not least because it looked as if at long last reparations from the Gelubba could be collected. The tally for reparations over very many years was carefully kept both in Turkana and Marsabit. By this time, the tally must have run into scores of thousands of cattle, sheep, goats and camels. In addition to thefts, a fixed amount of 'blood money' was added for every murder; fixed rates in head of stock, being recognised by custom for each man, woman and child. Frontier conferences in past years with the Italians and with the Ethiopian authorities before them, had seldom produced more than promises and aspirations of varying degrees of piety. These aspirations were sometimes quite genuine as far as the current ruling power was concerned but seldom had anyone succeeded in forcing the Gelubba to hand over as much as one scraggy goat. It now appeared to the Gabbra, Rendille and Turkana that the situation was almost too good to be true. And this indeed proved to be so.

In June, army support for a 'Gelubba war' seemed to be extremely strong; I say 'seemed' because although there was never any doubt about the genuine commitment at Brigade level for a major expedition, it became clear later that it had never been reviewed with any noticeable enthusiasm at higher command levels, if indeed it had been reviewed at all. I was authorised to raise one hundred tribal levies to go on with and enlistment day at North Horr produced scenes of great excitement. Fifty Rendille and fifty Gabbra young men were selected from the crowds of enthusiastic applicants. The successful men were issued with rifles and ammunition and given a little time to quieten down from the high state of exultation this engendered. several of them had thrown fits and were firmly sat on while they frothed at the mouth. The young warriors were given grave warnings about what would happen to them if they misbehaved or misused their weapons. Ba Allen then proceeded to give them some elementary training. The men were then allocated to selected Police N.C.O.'s who were made responsible for their further training and for nursing their charges pending the start of operations.

That night was a memorable one. Camp fires blazed in the desert around the North Horr military post and we ate our dinner to a strange medley of sound and smell. A hum of cheerful conversation was interrupted by snatches of song and the clickety-clack of rifle bolts as the proud owners put into practice the instructions they had been given for cleaning them. Occasionally, one could hear the liquid clonk-clonk of wooden bells as a new string of camels coming in from the desert padded momentarily into the firelight and all the time the familiar groaning and moaning of the hobbled camels already there. Over all of this, was the pervading, acrid stench of camel through which, every now and then, penetrated the glorious smell of roasting meat.

All this enthusiasm and preparation for war was for nothing. The first sign that we were living in a little world of our own was when we received a visit in July from the General Officer Commanding, East Africa Forces, General Sir Alan Cunningham. We very quickly discovered that he had not the slightest interest in our Gelubba war. He asked us if we knew there was another war taking place? Perhaps to emphasise this point, he told me at some length a story about a K.A.R. Company who had recently distinguished themselves when attacking an enemy position: they had lopped off the hand of each Italian as it appeared over the parapet. Eyeing me closely, he wondered if I was horrified. I suppose I was, being only a pseudo-soldier. What I would have liked to have said was that the Gelubba did not seem so efficient when they went for women and children but, unfortunately, I have only just thought of that now.

In August, the planned expedition against the Gelubba was officially cancelled. It was held that Emperor Haile Selassie was the authority now responsible for the good behaviour of the Gelubba tribe as a whole. There was one positive outcome; it was agreed that those Gelubba who lived in that part of the delta area which lay within the boundaries of the Marsabit District should come under the Marsabit administration. It was also agreed that a military post should be maintained for the time being at Ileret on the Lake shore, just south of Lug Banya, that we could move our Police posts to the northern wells and that we could disarm all Gelubba tribesmen living within our political boundaries as shown on the map. Like all half measures, these were to meet with only very limited success, at considerable expense in both effort and money.

Thus, it came about that the only opportunity which had ever occurred and was ever likely to occur, of putting the marauding Gelubba firmly in their place, was lost. I was left with the task of explaining to our own tribesmen why it was that, although we were capable of driving away enormous Italian forces which had never really done them any harm, we were quite incapable of dealing with a few thousand Gelubba at whose hands they and the Turkana had suffered grievous loss for several generations. Having long since concluded that we were an extremely illogical people, they accepted the situation with customary fatalism. However, I do not believe that the tribal levies which had been raised for offensive action with so much enthusiasm, ever really forgave us for relegating them to a purely defensive role.

(2)

Once it had became clear that the Italian retreat northwards was permanent, the inevitability of army withdrawal from the Northern Frontier District was something which had to be faced. Plans were put in place to substantially increase the strength of the Northern Frontier Division of the Kenya Police, on whom the whole task of frontier defence would then fall. The flower of Kenya's fighting tribes were already recruited into the K.A.R., or clamouring to be in it, so this exercise in expansion of the Police followed the pattern usual in such circumstances. Much of the human material available was second-hand and third rate; and some, you could say, was un-rateable. There was little time for adequate training, even if there had been the facilities for this. There were insufficient experienced officers and N.C.O.'s to handle such vastly increased numbers of recruits. Instead of being a small, efficient and tough police force of highly experienced regulars, who firmly and quite correctly believed that each of them was a match for any twenty raiders (we had one little Somali Corporal in Marsabit who on hearing news of a raid near the Hurri Hills, set off alone on a camel to cut the raiding party off – and in fact succeeded in rescuing some of the stolen stock), the force temporarily became an agglomeration of untrained men with rifles, big boots, little idea of what they were supposed to be doing and not much desire to do it. Few of them had any experience of the very tough conditions in which they had to operate. They were difficult to move and when they could be moved at all, it had to be in comparatively large units and only after going through the most cumbersome motions. However, it was bodies we mainly required; and it was only by a remarkable feat of recruitment and organisation on the part of the Kenya Police Headquarters that we were able to get them at all.

With the army now stationed at Ileret, albeit in a static role, the Lake shore raiding route of the Gelubba was successfully blocked. We reckoned that if we could also establish a strong

Police presence on the Buluk wells, from where the country eastwards to the Bukana post and westward to the Lake could be constantly patrolled, it should be possible to confine the Gelubba to their own area, or at least catch any raiding parties either coming in or as they returned across the border. By September, our Police strength was sufficient to make this plan practicable. I established a base at Darati, from which to launch the Buluk expeditionary force.

Following a few days spent in organising the safari, I was joined by Pat Whiting. He had replaced Ba Allen as head of the Marsabit police force. We set off with a motley group comprising thirty-six Kenya Police, four Tribal Police, fifty-two levies and various camel-leaders and others, bringing the total to one hundred and eighteen men. For transport, we had forty-four baggage camels, two riding camels and two three-ton trucks. The sixty-odd miles between Derati and Buluk consisted of very broken terrain although mostly open or covered with only light bush. We had no idea how far we could travel with the trucks as there was no road to follow. We set off, identifying the route to follow as we went. Progress was difficult and tortuous; but it is remarkable how far you can take trucks in such broken up countryside if you go slowly enough.

The tribal levies were still rankling under the decision not to use them as part of an aggressive force in the delta against the Gelubba. During some elementary field exercises I had held for them while encamped at Derati, they had released some of their suppressed feelings on the Tribal Police 'enemy'. Not being satisfied with the theoretical capture of their opponents, they went to great lengths to truss them up so soundly that their release took quite some time to effect. The Tribal Police took great umbrage at such undignified treatment and feelings between the two bodies were strained for a couple of days.

We camped that evening at Lug Namja which we found to be at quite a different location from where it was marked on the map. After standing-to at 4.30 next morning, we moved off at 7 a.m. and camped again at 1 p.m. We selected a site from which

THE GLITTERING LAKE

we could readily make a reconnaissance of the Buluk wells. Our most up-to-date intelligence information said that there was a concentration of Gelubba in the area. We had, however, misjudged the distance and a scouting party under Pat Whiting, which had left at 3 p.m., did not return until dark and having failed to reach Buluk. Whilst they had seen no signs of Gelubba, they had found a suitable line of country for our motor transport which had come under a great deal of difficulty during the past ten miles.

Next morning, we again set off at 7 a.m. on the last leg of the journey. By noon, our advance party had reached the wells and found them deserted. The main force arrived an hour later. The trucks and rear-guard staggered in at 5 p.m. in the afternoon having had to push, haul and coax the trucks most of the way. The Buluk wells, of which there were nine, were strung out along the edge of a dry watercourse. They were bored through solid rock, some to depths of thirty feet. These wells, therefore, were deeply quarried crevices. Water was drawn from them by means of leather buckets, usually made from giraffe, and which were passed from hand to hand up the steep sides by men perched precariously in suitable niches. In this, they were identical to several other wells in the Northern Frontier area. The making of these wells is ascribed to various earlier people, most notably to a tall race called the Maanthinle about which no records remain. The excavation of these wells, using only hand tools of some kind, must have been a very difficult and time-consuming task; certainly, none of the existing tribes could ever have made them nor did they make any such claim. What was perhaps even more remarkable was the way in which they had been sited. There was no trace of a series of unsuccessful borings, denoting a long period of trial and error; and at Buluk, as at other sites, there seemed to be no obvious reasons for having decided that water would necessarily be found on the actual sites chosen. In comparatively recent times, the Samburu frequented the area as far north as Buluk but were pushed out by those migrating down from the north. A Boran told me that the place was so named because when a Boran raiding party was approaching many years ago, they heard an old man softly calling to his goats in the dark, "Buluk – Buluk – Buluk" and the name stuck.

We chose a good site for a Police post, from which the wells could be easily commanded. There was a fine view of the surrounding countryside even though this meant it was rather too exposed to the perpetual gale that swept across the broken desert terrain. Next morning, we laid out the foundations in the shape of an equilateral triangle with semi-circular redoubts at each angle and began the process of building the walls with the loose larval rocks lying around in unlimited quantities. By the afternoon, it was beginning to take on the appearances of a small fort and we took time off for a brief occupation ceremony. After all, we were hoisting the flag in what may
well have been the last officially unoccupied and un-administered piece of British territory in Africa, certainly in East Africa and we recognised our responsibilities as the last of the Empire Builders. We could not but regret that the piece of Empire we were building was as unprepossessing and inhospitable as any in which the King's writ ran. As we hoisted the flag, we

Figure 29: (top) Marsabit: Tribal Police mule patrol, (bottom) in the heart of the Hurri Hills.

felt it a great pity that the King's new subjects were nowhere to be seen. It was also all too clear that if we wished to keep the flag flying, literally, we would have to supply the outpost with far more flags than our meagre financial resources could possibly afford. Previous experience tended to show that the Kenya Treasury included any such symbols under the heading of T.U.E. (Totally Unjustified Expenditure).

(3)

We listed the various stores and materials that needed to be despatched to Buluk on our return to Marsabit. We installed a suitable garrison, left instructions for the completion of the post and Standing Orders for the N.C.O. in charge. We then set off for Ileret with the remainder of the party. Ileret, on the Lake shore, was now the site of a military post manned by a Company of the 1st Northern Rhodesia Regiment. We arrived after an eight-hour struggle with our two trucks but felt considerably elated at having proved that the construction of a motorable track to connect these outposts with distant Marsabit was quite practicable.

After the dry barrenness of the country we had been through, it was a joy to be back beside the Lake and to sit down to a supper of fresh Tilapia fish which tasted as good as any food I have ever eaten. We happened to arrive on a day the troops had laid on an elaborate evening of entertainment and it was midnight before we made our way to our camp beds, exhausted but with feelings of contentment. The troops were mainly drawn from a tribe called Yao and their homes in Nyasaland[8] were a considerable distance away. Their singing and drumming were magnificent, the kind of deep throated and rhythmic music that only Africa can produce; even now, as I recall that night, I feel shivers running through my body. In addition to the songs, there was a series of topical sketches in which few holds were barred. Wave upon wave of tumultuous laughter rumbled across the waters of the Lake, glistening coldly under a rising moon.

THE GLITTERING LAKE

Next day, we travelled north for thirteen miles, to Bani, where a meeting with Chief Lokwaria and his Gelubba elders had been hastily arranged. This was the first time we had come face to face with the Gelubba, whose very name personified terror amongst the other local tribes in the Northern Frontier District. It was somehow disappointing, therefore, to find that they looked so mild and inoffensive and in no way different from our own people. The tribe they most closely resembled was the Turkana; but even amongst the small numbers present, the mixed origins of the Gelubba could be seen in the variety of features and skin colour. They had already ingratiated themselves with the Army who now considered them excellent fellows. As I walked across the dusty ground to the meeting from my truck, I found that much of the sternness and anger I had been storing up for this meeting had already begun to evaporate.

My official interpreter was a young Somali called Hussein. He and two Gabbra Tribal Policemen had accompanied us in the truck. I noticed that the two Gabbra were no longer with us and I asked Hussein where they were.

"They are over there," he said, pointing back towards the truck.

I followed the direction of his finger and saw one of them standing with his arms clasped around his chest and head down, next to the truck. The other man was lying on the ground, a white bundle of cloth, topped by the red patch of his turban. I turned back to Hussein. "What the hell are they doing?" I began. Before I had time to say or do anything more, Hussein broke in across me.

"They have an ague, sir. The sight of the Gelubba has made them so upset and angry that unless they can shudder it off, they may do something terrible."

It was true enough. The two Tribal Policemen were foaming at the mouth and were in no fit state to do anything. As they had their rifles with them, I was glad they had come no further.

How difficult it must have been for our local tribesmen

to understand our British way of arranging matters. To us, the smiling, ordinary-looking Gelubba, the 'excellent fellows' who sold eggs and chickens and carried out various menial chores for the Army and some of whom had been wandering peaceably around the Army camp when we arrived, were now deemed eminently suitable for inclusion under the protective umbrella of our colonial administration. However, to the two Gabbra policemen, they were the people who for generations and up to only a few months ago, had been massacring their women and children and plundering their livestock. Here we were, come to sit down and talk with them, instead of lining them up along the Lake shore and shooting them. The Gelubba continued to look harmless but I found some of the sternness and anger seeping back into my mind.

What I said to the Gelubba Chief and his elders, I now cannot recall; but I know the Army thought it both mean and uncalled for. This I discovered six months later when the Army evacuated Ileret and left their records in my office and the Gelubba once more to their own devices. According to the records, my speech did not consist of a hearty welcome into our great family of nations. It was, indeed, very difficult to say anything specific, as we could not yet tell whether our occupation of this corner of the delta was to be permanent or not. The Gelubba, for their part, must have been more polite, or at least shown a determination not to retreat from the 'excellent fellows' position they had created. A short, naïve note in my diary records: "An historic day in that the last independent tribe in Kenya Colony (perhaps in British Africa) accepted our rule."

Chief Lokwaria took no active role in our proceedings. He was a very frail man and remained under a shelter, paying little attention, even to the flies which swarmed over his emaciated body. He greeted me cheerfully enough and recalled Count Teleki's visit in 1888 which he assured me he remembered quite vividly. He continued to remark that my coming was merely a prophesy fulfilment, almost to the day, which had been made by a wise old man at the time. That was, I quickly calculated, only fifty-three years ago. As Lokwaria was then a young man, he must now be some seventy years old, a ripe old age in those parts.

A little over six months later, it became necessary for the Ileret army post to be withdrawn. We had not yet the means to establish a permanent Police post of a size adequate for such an isolated and vulnerable place, being some 250 very long and difficult miles from Marsabit. We managed to maintain Buluk - but our Lake shore defences were once more back at Alia Bay.

Within ten days of the evacuation of Ileret, the Gelubba were back at their old ways. Raiders attacked a road gang as far south as Lug Bulal, sixty miles from the frontier. The six-month occupation did prove, however, that the best means of controlling the Gelubba was to have a strong force deposited right inside their doorstep. More than two years were to pass before such a policy finally received Government approval and some time longer before it was possible for the policy to be made effective. As it happened, it was approved only two or three days before I departed from the Northern Frontier District for good.

(4)

If the occupation of Ileret proved one thing, its evacuation proved another – how useless were temporary palliatives, although a breathing space had been engendered in which the creation of an expanded Police unit could proceed. In the eighteen months immediately following the army withdrawal, Gelubba raids accounted for the death of another sixty or more Gabbra and the loss of considerable numbers of livestock. The abandonment of the proposed delta expedition had forced the Gabbra to the conclusion that any redress would have to come from them. As a result, an unprecedented number of counter-raids took place, in which thirty or forty Gelubba were said to have been killed, but quite possibly were not. A situation developed in which raid and counter-raid tumbled along in quick succession. It became clear that sentimental feelings in support of our own 'side' had to be firmly suppressed. If not, the continuous shedding of blood would become the normal state of affairs, in which without a doubt our tribesmen would inevitably suffer the most. The alternative would have been to abandon the use of more than half the District. Of course, this alternative would not have been much of a solution: inadequate water and grazing would have compelled the Gabbra and Rendille to encroach on the preserves of their southern and western neighbours, while the areas open to raiding would have been further extended into the very heart of the District, rather than being confined to the north.

The years 1942 and 1943 must have been amongst the worst ever, as far as raiding was concerned, for the whole of the Northern Frontier District. These two years also saw the introduction of a new feature to the raiding: the staging of deliberate and organised attacks on Police posts, an unheard-of situation in pre-war days. Several organised gangs of well-armed bandits were operating to the east of Marsabit; the most notorious under a Somali called Mur Kanyere made successful raids deep into the Moyale and Mandera Districts. It was not until late in 1943 that this gang leader was killed whilst attacking a Police patrol.

It was fortunate that by April 1942, a long, drawn-out debate concerning the arming of the Northern Frontier Division of the Kenya Police with automatic weapons was finally resolved in favour of doing so. In that month, the first ex-Italian Breda guns arrived and training in their use immediately started. These weapons proved not too effective at first: when the Police post at Karsa had the first real chance to use its Breda gun, it, of course, jammed. The Corporal in charge is probably still running through his extensive vocabulary of expletives, wringing his hands and muttering: "They were right in our sights, right in our sights." However, the psychological effect of these weapons was considerable from the very start. It was also at this time decided to issue all Police and administrative officers with the Sten gun. The personnel concerned were obliged to carry this weapon when travelling in the frontier areas. If these decisions had been made a little sooner, many lives, including several British lives, may well have been saved. One of these British lives lost was a close friend and contemporary of mine.

Willie Keir was a short, mild but fundamentally very tough Scotsman. He was one of eleven of us who came to Kenya as District Officers (Cadet) in 1935. Following a notably successful wartime tour of duty as District Commissioner, Wajir (the most Beau Geste-like of all the frontier stations), Willie was chosen for the job of re-opening the Mandera station. His task was to re-establish our administration in that District after it was vacated by the Italians at the time of their general retreat. It was a very disturbed, lawless area but following the signing of a treaty with Ethiopia in January 1942, things quietened down, apart from the occasional raid by one of several gangs of professional bandits from across the border. These gangs mostly consisted of ex-Italian Somali troops. The tribesmen had hopes that they might now succeed in receiving some compensation for their losses in life and livestock during the previous eighteen months. In March, however, the lull came to an end. Feuds between Moslems and Pagans started in Ethiopia and refugees once more came streaming across the border into Kenya.

Figure 30: (top) Rendille women moving house, (bottom) evening at a small Rendille encampment.

Figure 31: (top) Mega: the Round House, (bottom) Mega: Gerald Reece presenting a medal to a Kenya Police sergeant attached to the South African Forces with Ba Allen watching.

Figure 32: (top) Marsabit: Bonham's Shifta sorting ammunition for an air drop, (bottom) removing mines on the Mega-Yavello road.

THE GLITTERING LAKE

Figure 33: (top) K.A.R. convoy entering Yavello, (bottom) occupation of Yavello: hoisting the Union Jack flag.

Figure 34: (top) raising Gabbra and Rendille tribal levies at North Horr (Ba Allen in foreground), (bottom) Breda guns arrive for the police: the author trying out the new toy.

The situation was ideal for the professional bandits and on the 21st April, while on safari with a small escort of ten policemen, Willie received news of one of their raids. He immediately despatched a patrol of five men to reconnoitre the area and sent a runner to Mandera for reinforcements. The patrol encountered a handful of raiders driving off camels and opened fire. The raiders dispersed and a party of local tribesmen nipped in to recover their stock. Hearing of the incident and fearing that his small patrol might run into serious trouble, Willie Keir collected his remaining five men and with a local elder as guide, went to their assistance with all speed. Unfortunately, he did not succeed in joining forces with them. In thick bush, he suddenly found himself confronted by the main gang of raiders who, not knowing the strength of their original adversaries, were making a flanking movement to avoid further fire from that patrol. That patrol, unaware that reinforcements were arriving, had meanwhile withdrawn. Willie's small party stood their ground and attempted to shoot it out against vastly superior numbers but gradually they were surrounded. Willie was shot in the back at about ten yards range and Sergeant Elmi, two constables and the guide were also killed. The raiders made off with their wounded and about fifteen hundred camels. This number of camels was subsequently estimated to have been only half the amount the raiders would have succeeded in looting had Willie's party not intervened.

Willie Keir was awarded, posthumously, the King's Commendation for Gallantry and the two surviving policemen who had fought their way out only after it was clear that their comrades were beyond help, were awarded the Colonial Police Medal for Gallantry.

I was in Nairobi on the 22 April, on my way back to Marsabit after some local leave, when I heard the news. Gerald rang me at the New Stanley Hotel. "They've got Willie," was all he said. The larger enemy had got Willie's brother only a few months previously.

Thirty-one of us who had served with him erected a modest memorial tablet in Willie's family church in Angus, Scotland, so far from the dusty spot where lay his body, from the life that he had led and loved and from the clop-clop of the camel bells where the great herds moved majestically across the desert plains. The tablet read:
'In affectionate memory of
William Keir Kenya Administrative Service
Who was killed in action on the 21 April, 1942
Near Gadeir on the Ethiopian frontier whilst
Fighting for the protection of British tribesmen.
For his bravery on this occasion, he was
Posthumously commended by His Majesty the King.
Erected by his brother officers'.

(5)

In July 1943, work took me to Moyale which I had not seen since a few days after its re-occupation in 1941. British Moyale stood at some 3500 feet above sea level, on the southern side of an east-west valley; Ethiopian Moyale faced it from the opposite slope. The international boundary was assumed to run down the valley between the two towns. A new Governor of Borana Province, Colonel Asfrau Walde Giorgis, had recently assumed office and I was informed it was my duty to call on him officially. I had not been expecting this formal occasion and the best I could manage in the way of formal clothes was a worn pair of flannel slacks, a borrowed and rather too large tweed jacket and somebody's old school tie.

Not ever having experienced one before, I was appalled to find a substantial guard of honour drawn up outside the Governor's official but very temporary Residence. I need not have worried because the troops had clearly never handled one either. All parties concerned eventually got through the ceremony which, by general consent, was deemed to be finished as soon as each participant had completed, to his own satisfaction, the motions he had previously decided to be the most appropriate to the occasion. We then retired to Colonel Asfrau's sitting-room for refreshments. Now whiskey was as rare as rain in the N.F.D. and the gallant Colonel's hand was heavy. Within five minutes, he had claimed most of our frontier wells for his Emperor. I countered with the suggestion that as His Imperial Majesty had shown such deep concern for his subjects in the Borana Province as to place their affairs in the hands of the only person he could trust to handle them with justice, wisdom and modern standards of efficiency, it might now be possible for some form of elementary administrative control to be exercised in the south-west part of what we readily agreed to be his territory.

"I will arrange it," he assured me.

I then suggested that as he was going to occupy the area, we might hold an official meeting to be attended by representative elders of Gabbra, Rendille and Gelubba to discuss compensation for our tribesmen for the losses they had suffered over so many years; against which, of course, would be set off any claims against them.

"I will arrange it," said Colonel Asfrau.

By the time we had reached the last two fingers in the bottle, Colonel Asfrau had successfully arranged everything we could think of, so I took my leave and was wafted down the hill and up the other side on a cushion of alcohol and good fellowship. I was determined to arrange to spend the next twelve hours in bed.

This arrangement, in common with all the others, never materialised. At 7.30 p.m., a signaller brought a message from a police post east of Moyale, stating that Nur Kanyere and his gang were in the area. Information had been received that they planned to ambush Gerald Reece on his way back to Moyale from Mandere the following day.

The Moyale Police were heavily pre-occupied with other issues and only a handful remained in the station. Resident there, however, was Hugh Grant who had served many years in the Northern Frontier administration. He had recently been designated British Consul at Mega. Grant was in the process of recruiting and training his Consular guard, prior to taking up his appointment. As ex-British Army, ex-Black and Tan, ex-K.A.R. and ex-commander of his own group of local Irregulars (which had only recently been disbanded), Hugh Grant was an expert in bush warfare. He was training his new unit along lines so unorthodox that it caused near apoplexy to every police and army officer with whom he came into contact.

Hugh was unorthodox in many other ways, too. His favourite after-dinner pastime was shooting matchboxes off the mantle-piece. With a revolver, he prided himself on being quick on the draw. In a situation, his inclination was to bring about an immediate conclusion rather than exercising diplomacy and patience, therefore he had never endeared himself to normal down-country administration. Having successfully survived two major and several minor wars, one revolution and several frontier skirmishes, it was an unkind fate which a few years later decided he was to end his life transfixed by the spear of an angry young warrior at a cattle sale in Masailand. Hugh, at that time, was in charge of the Masai extra-Provincial District. It was a tragedy for him and his family – and, also, the Masai. Those who knew Hugh well could never have envisaged such an end to his life. As is sometimes the case with such people, when he was not being stubborn or quick-tempered, Hugh was the soul of kindness to others. I first met him when I was packing my kit prior to travelling to Lodwar. He noticed I was lacking any weapon for such a wild place (the salary of a District officer with two years was then £400 per year). He immediately presented me with a .32 Colt revolver, his excuse being that it was of no use, anyhow. To prove this, he told me a story of a young probationary American gangster. This man, who possessed a Colt revolver, was told by an old hand that he would be wise to file down the fore sight. On asking why he should mutilate such a fine weapon in this way, the old hand replied: "It's quite dangerous to have a fore sight on such a toy, son, very dangerous indeed. Because one day you'll point it at someone - and he'll just be very amused. He'll take the gun off you and he'll – well, son, you know what he'll do. Much better you get that fore sight filed off quick, son."

From the most recent information on the movements of Nur Kanyere's gang, Hugh Grant estimated its present likely position. There was just a chance that they would use a certain track which cut across the Moyale-Mandera road about 18 miles east of Moyale. If we left Moyale at about 11 p.m., we would reach that place at the best time to lay an ambush, taking a chance that these calculations were correct.

We set off in three trucks with a force consisting of forty consular guards and fifteen Police and Tribal Police, including my own small, Marsabit detachment. Hugh's organisation and tactics were impressive; and we positioned our forces with a minimum of confusion. Of course, Nur Kanyere and his gang never materialised but for some moments just before dawn, an old man leading three camels down the track was in grave danger. He gave us some allegedly first- hand information (which subsequently proved to be correct), that the gang was much further east and the previous day had attacked a Police post.

At 6.30 a.m., we set off on foot eastwards determined to make the best job possible of clearing the road. Patrols fanned out into the bush on either side, investigating every possible hide-out. By the time we set up camp at 6.30 p.m. that evening, we had searched more than thirty miles of road verge. Gerald Reece turned up two hours later, unscathed, and with information about an action between a police patrol and part of Nur Kanyere's gang still further to the east. It was believed that the gang had now retreated across the frontier border.

Figure 35: (top) Derati Hill and police post, (bottom) on the summit of Derati Hill, interpreter Hussein standing.

Figure 36: (top) on the way to Buluk, (bottom) loading up after a mid-day halt.

Figure 37: (top) breaking camp at dawn on the way to Buluk, Pat Whiteing dressing, (bottom) sunrise near Buluk, taken from the author's camp bed.

Figure 38: (top) Buluk: occupation ceremony in the foundations of the new post, (bottom) Buluk: thinking about how to build the new post.

Figure 39: (top) Bani: Chief Lokwaria of the Eastern Gelubba, (bottom) Bani: an assortment of Gelubba.

THE GLITTERING LAKE

Figure 40: (top) Tribal Police and ostrich nest, (bottom) not Lake Rudolf but the Chelbi Desert flooded after rain (taken from the running board of a lorry stranded in the middle of it).

Thirty miles on top of Colonel Asfrau's whiskey proved to be the best possible sleeping draught. We were picked up next morning by truck and arrived back in Moyale to hear the news of allied landings in Sicily. It was just the kind of news which Hugh Grant needed to set him off on a display of superb marksmanship.

CHAPTER EIGHT

OCCASIONS AND REFLECTIONS

(1)

'My flesh looketh for Thee in a dry and thirsty land where no water is'. I do not think that anyone who has not lived in desert country and been in daily contact with nomadic people can ever really appreciate the true significance of many biblical allusions – even, or perhaps especially, those familiar since childhood. I was brought up, at times reluctantly, on the well-known Psalms of David. I had not been in the Lake Rudolph region long before the once-familiar phrases began to bubble up into my consciousness with a completely unrealised wealth of meaning and imagery. The cries and longings of the psalmist sprang into vivid reality against their proper background; as in the first moment of success when the unaccustomed hand jiggles a pair of aerial photographs under a stereoscope. In the black, barren landscape of the Dida Galgalla, I took a personal and passionate interest in the promise that 'the sun shall not strike thee by day' and many a time, as I plodded my way homewards across the Chelbi, I lifted my eyes unto the approaching hills and watched the forested cap of Marsabit mountain draw nearer and greener as the miles passed, with deep joy and thankfulness. The exquisite pleasures of shade, of green pastures, of a shower of rain, of new life bursting from the dead ground, of a camp near a clear pool when the sun has just set and the stars begin to burn so fiercely that one feels they might explode. These wonders are hidden from the inexperienced, as is the shock of unbelief engendered by that ultimate in miracles – the gush of clear water bursting from the barren rock - which I have witnessed with my own eyes.

Again I, for one, had never previously thought that there was much to that phrase 'a cup of cold water', which had previously only conjured up vague images of a prison diet. I used to think of water as something that came out of a tap (if I ever thought of it at all), although quite ready to laugh patronisingly at jokes about slum evacuees thinking that milk was something which came out of a tin or bottle. My recollection of the mental image that particular phrase used to produce for me is that there was included not only a tap (large, brass) but also a willow-pattern cup. It took experience of the desert to teach me what a priceless gift a cup of really cold water can be. Wells, too, used to be coloured in my mind by the illustrations commonly associated with 'Jack and Jill' and 'Ding Dong Bell' in nursery rhyme books. Whatever may be the case in other deserts, in the northern deserts of Kenya the average waterhole or well was generally a stinking mess, unless you were lucky enough to be the first person to use it for a very long time (in which case it would either have become filled in, be stagnant or be a clear pool with a running trickle of water, according to type). Where shallow wells were dug seasonally in sand riverbeds, one or more of a group was normally set aside for domestic purposes, including drinking. All this meant, in practice, was that the domestic water supply was not so noticeably impregnated as the others with the urine of the countless camels, cattle, sheep or goats which daily surrounded them. To me, the worst form of pollution was undoubtedly baboon, whose peculiar stink made a bath just as nauseating as one taken at the most expensive of medicinal spas without any of the compensating curative effects. For internal use, neither boiling or filtering nor the addition of whiskey could ever quite remove its penetrating and uniquely distinctive odour.

The Boran, Rendille and Gabbra normally watered their stock in troughs built up with puddled mud near the waterhole or made from hollowed Dom palm logs if these were available. The origins of most of the deep, permanent wells drilled through rock which were found in certain places have been lost in the mists of time; but other deep wells were excavated annually. Depths were reckoned by the number of men and girls required to draw water, one above the other, passing leather buckets, often made from giraffe skins, up and down with quite incredible rapidity for hours on end and maintaining a rhythm with a simple, monotonous chant. It was not unusual for a deep well to have bends and angles in its passage and it's hard to imagine what it must have been like for those unfortunate to be at or near the bottom. A human chain of twelve or more people underground was necessary in some wells and I have been told up to twenty occasionally. More frequently, however, three or four would suffice. I never had the courage to explore the interior of the more complicated well. Apart from the fact that I doubted my ability to perform the required acrobatics, the claustrophobic effect could have been comparable to only that experienced in inching one's way through a narrow, escape tunnel from a prisoner-of-war camp.

The standard means of keeping drinking water cool whilst on safari was the well-known and universally used canvas water bag, holding about a gallon. In a dry climate and especially one in which a strong, hot wind is normal, water cools rapidly through the evaporation effect in these handy porous containers which can be carried by hand or slung over the saddle of a mule or camel, or hung from a car or truck – or even from a tree branch, tent pole or tripod of sticks when in camp. In the station, we used charcoal coolers or porous earthenware vessels, both of which were very efficient if properly looked after. The best safari water cooler I ever had was one which I devised myself. This consisted of a large ex-Italian aluminium water bottle acquired in Mega and which I covered with the thick felt padding used under a saddle. Before setting out on safari, the felt-covered bottle was soaked in water for about five minutes and then slung from truck or camel. A walk of half an hour (or shorter if driving) was sufficient to lower the water temperature to what, by comparison, felt ice-cold. I came to regard this simple piece of equipment as my dearest possession.

(2)

It is only when, for some reason, we suddenly find ourselves without them, that we realise how much we have come to rely on certain basic inventions which we accept without question. There is nothing more commonplace than a box of matches but there was a time in Marsabit when a box was as scarce as gold and almost as scarce as beer. It was not too difficult to keep a fire going in a house or in a fixed camp but running out of matches when you were, perhaps, a ten-day march from home could be trying. Rubbing sticks together may be a good enough game for Boy Scouts and, although many of the tribesmen were experts, even they preferred, when possible, to carry fire with them when they were on the move – just a few smouldering embers in a special container. On several occasions, I have carried a lighted hurricane lantern for days on end, having plenty of oil but no matches.

In the sort of conditions which prevailed in the Turkana and Marsabit Districts, we quickly learned to improvise when things went wrong; and to make as certain as possible beforehand that they would not go wrong. Even in the stations, we had to rely much on our own very limited resources. True, we had roads connecting us with civilisation - but these were all dirt roads and rain could make them impassable for weeks, sometimes for months. We had, indeed, radio sets - but these spent much of the time out of action for one reason or another. Aircraft were

THE GLITTERING LAKE

Figure 41: Beside still waters.

theoretically available but only in case of grave emergency (the term 'grave' in the context did indeed mean that some unfortunate person was just about in one); and provided your landing-strip was in a suitable condition to receive aircraft. We had a medical officer at Lodwar and a sub-assistant surgeon at Lokitaung but treatment and medicines were very basic. While the Army was present at Marsabit, we had all kinds of army medical staff, field hospital and ambulance facilities; but on the Army's departure, we reverted to the civil establishment of one African Nursing Orderly, one grade up from African Dresser which was the lowest grade. The Medical Department boasted one Medical Officer in the Northern Frontier District, an area of approximately 90,000 square miles. He was stationed at Wajir; to reach Marsabit involved a road journey of some 450 miles, if the road was passable. As can be imagined, we did not see much of him. Our nearest Medical officer was in fact stationed at Meru, some 240 miles to the south but outside the boundaries of the Northern Frontier.

Under such circumstances, administrative and police officers became quite experienced general medical practitioners out of necessity and the safari medicine chest was a very important item. The contents of this chest reflected not only the statistical forecast of probable accidents and ailments but also the owner's imaginative faculties and his own assessment of his abilities in all fields of medical science. There being no wonder-drugs at that time, it was not possible to make a blanket diagnosis and treat for the worst possible case in the knowledge that it would very probably cure any of the most likely. On the other hand, we possessed few drugs which could do much serious harm and when stumped on the diagnosis, belief in our medical infallibility was so widespread that a mixture of Epsom salts and aspirin, to which might be added a few traces of iodine, permanganate and such like (according to what seemed intuitively right at the time), all mixed together with a strong dose of faith, could and very frequently did, work miracles. Although I fancied myself medically in no small way and had my own fixed ideas on medical practice, I was never able to compete with a colleague who preceded me in Turkana. Quite unused to local conditions, he was suddenly landed with a terrible case on his first safari: he successfully delivered a Turkana woman of a stillborn baby that had been dead in its mother's womb for over a week. My main contribution to unqualified medical practice was the curing of an allegedly bewitched Gabbra child who had not, I think, spoken for two days and had been deemed to have been struck permanently dumb. I administered a concoction of vividly coloured fruit salts to the accompaniment of suitable noisy incantations, followed up by various detailed instructions on the aftercare to the highly impressed parents.

The only serious illness I had during these years occurred when I was on local leave down-country and, apart from a few bouts of malaria and 'flu, I enjoyed perfect health. Nor did I experience any accidents on safari, not even a sprained ankle while traversing the dangerously sharp and loose larva rock which covered a significant portion of the Marsabit District. Indeed, apart from the inevitable hold-ups in mud, floods or sand, the only notable safari incidents in which I was involved were the over-turning of my truck in heavy rain, a camel-leader being bitten by a snake and a guide who was walking in front on one occasion in the Harri Hills practically falling over a sleeping leopard; and none of these had any serious consequences. If I was fortunate at the time in not attracting misfortune, I greatly miss it now.

Our African Nursing Orderly had to cope as best he could with whatever came his way and very well he did it. His only option was to send a patient down to the hospital in Meru, if by good luck transport happened to be available. On one occasion, he was called out to deal with a situation resulting from a red Italian 'pillar-box' bomb exploding in a Boran hut. A young goat herder had found it and after playing with this attractive toy for a few hours, he became tired of it and threw it into the fire. Two members of the family were killed immediately; and four others suffered terrible injuries. These latter the Nursing Orderly dealt with single-handed and in a manner later described as one which would do credit to the Casualty Department of a London hospital. We radioed for the Medical Officer from Meru; but he only got half-way in two days, almost killing himself from thirst and starvation in the process. With the best of intentions but being only used to 'Kenya' conditions as opposed to 'Northern Frontier' conditions, he had set out in his car with one bottle of water and a packet of mutton-and-mustard sandwiches. He burst two tyres after only travelling seventy miles and was immobilised. He had failed either to let us know that he had left Meru or to check in on the way through Isiolo. Consequently, we knew nothing about his misfortunes until we received a message from him after he had been picked up by chance and returned to Meru in rather poor condition. We managed to transport the injured patients to hospital and two of them recovered but it was too late for the other two who had, in the meantime, contracted tetanus.

(3)

Doreen joined me in Marsabit in June, 1941. No (comparatively) newly-weds could have set up house in more charming surroundings. When Rosemary Whiteing shortly afterwards joined her husband Pat in the Police house next door, life in

Marsabit began to take on quite a civilized air, the all-pervading army camp atmosphere being diluted if not entirely dissipated.

The main room of the District Commissioner's house was thatched, with whitewashed walls and black timbered window frames and beams, giving it an authentic 'ye olde English' appearance. Bits and pieces had subsequently been added on by various previous occupiers who had been more concerned with utility than aesthetics. There was now a fair-sized bedroom with bathroom at one end and a block of two very small bedrooms at the other, all built of stones with corrugated iron roofs. These annexes were partly overgrown with creepers so were not such eyesores as they might sound. Each of them had been a financial wangle (the only source of even the most modest kind of amenity in such places in those days) but no one had ever succeeded in wangling enough to install any form of indoor sanitation. The 'other offices' were represented by a deep-pit latrine in a small grass rondavel at the bottom of the garden, to reach which in the mud and mist of Marsabit was sometimes a major operation, to be mounted with care and foresight. The final piece of drill was to make sure you ducked your head as you entered to preserve your eyes from the attention of any spitting cobra who might by chance have installed itself in the thatch over the door.

Although Marsabit, at 4,500 feet above sea level, had a climate in common elsewhere in Kenya at about 7,000 feet, water was always a real problem. For much of the year, the township supply had to be strictly rationed and when this rationed supply dried up, water had to be carted long distances. Any form of piped supply was unheard off. The nearest stream of unarguably adequate size was some eleven miles away, deep in the forest, so the expense involved was a very real obstacle to progress. Nevertheless, the bi-annual dry-weather water exercise was a nightmare. The human population of Marsabit was expanding rapidly, especially the Police unit, improvisation was becoming less and less successful and we were becoming genuinely desperate. I put forward a modest proposal that a small and awkwardly located spring about three-quarters of a mile above the town, near the small, forest crater of Sokorte Dikka, should be run into a pipe and gravitated down; but the estimated cost of about £900 was considered prohibitive. These were before the days of widespread Colonial development and Welfare Projects financed by the United Kingdom Government – or, anyhow, before the days when it was deemed that either welfare or development had much relevance to places like Marsabit. We collected, of course, what rainwater we could but as nearly all roofs were thatched – and sizeable water tanks in any case cost a great deal of money – supplies from this source were very limited. For part of the year, Marsabit was one of the wettest places we have lived in; but it was, nevertheless, the place where water-consciousness was burned deep into our souls. It took quite some time for Doreen and me to get used to not sharing our bathwater when we went down country; and even today, I cannot put more than three fingers of water in my tooth mug without a conscious effort and a subsequent feeling of guilt.

An unusually long dry season in 1942 brought matters to a head. By this time, not only had the Police unit reached the unprecedented total of one hundred and forty men but the town population was back to pre-war normality. It became either a matter of getting more water or evacuating the station. In September, a survey of the Sokorte Dikka scheme was made and although the estimated daily yield was small, no other remedy was possible save at impossible expense. The materials duly arrived and construction commenced. Fortunately, we had been able to reduce the cost to a minimum by finding an ex-military steel storage tank in the forest. This we dismantled and brought into the station, together with various other useful scraps picked up in a systematic rummage of all the old military camp sites, now practically obliterated by new forest growth.

The construction team consisted of a Sikh technician and two African fitters. The Sikh was an excellent fellow - but he thought little of Marsabit and that little he expressed in picturesque language. He thought even less of it when he ran into a buffalo on his first day's visit to the spring. It took us several days to cajole and wheedle him into any sort of mental state adequate to the reasonably efficient performance of his allotted task. A most happy compromise was reached whereby he undertook to complete the job in record time; and we undertook to deploy a squad of armed guards along the pipeline.

I can recall no more exciting and satisfying event than the turning-on of the water supply a few weeks later. To see and hear clean water frothing under high pressure into the tank at the back of the house moved us all to tears: huge crowds of African women and their families clack-clacked and ah-ahed as they gathered round the standpipes in the police lines. Those people from down-country were excited enough but to many of the locals, the idea of obtaining water by the simple expediency of turning on a tap fixed to the end of a piece of piping was so utterly sophisticated and remarkable as to be beyond comprehension. Our joy, however, was short-lived; a few days later the elephants decided that they were not going to be deprived of what had been a most convenient supply for them and they launched an all-out assault. While one party of elephants damaged the reservoir by trying to drink out of it, another ripped down the spring-head installations. This battle continued intermittently, with limited successes claimed by both sides as cunning move was met by super-cunning counter move. We did not achieve final victory until we had dug a massive elephant proof moat round the reservoir and had fortified the installations at the spring in-take to an extent which would have kept out a brigade of heavy tanks.

(4)

On the night of the 22nd March 1942, our daughter Alison was born in Nairobi, to the accompaniment of a severe thunderstorm which knocked out the Nursing Home's electricity supply. Fortunately, an electric torch was found and a successful delivery was made. Three weeks later, I drove the station truck down from Marsabit to Nairobi, managing to combine its annual overhaul with family transport. After a stay of ten days, we set out on the return journey, Doreen and Alison taking the train as far as Nanyuki.

We had planned a pre-prepared camp at the Merille River crossing, some ninety miles north of Isiolo, to break the journey, on the assumption that we would arrive at a reasonable time. However, it was five o'clock in the afternoon before we managed to leave Isiolo in convoy with a trader's truck, several hours later than we had intended. Baby Alison travelled in a carrycot in the front of the truck, on the knees of Joy Percival (who was to stay for a couple of weeks with us in Marsabit, to initiate us into the mysteries of managing a baby) which I was driving. Doreen followed in the second truck. We arrived at the Merille camp at 11.30 pm to find the camp ready but a nasty, muddy mess as there had been heavy rain. To add to our general discomfort, a herd of elephant rumbled and snorted round us for most of what remained of the night which for all of us, except Alison who took it in her stride, was not restful.

Progress next morning was very slow, for the river had come down in flood; but after a few setbacks we eventually succeeded in crossing and ploughed a slow track northwards. At the northern end of the Kaisut, we came to a sudden stop, for northbound and southbound military convoys (using the now regular supply route through the Hurri Hills) had become inextricably mixed and skidded three-tonners were littered about the road at all angles. It was by now midday, the sun was blistering hot and Doreen was attempting to feed a very hungry Alison without any privacy from the military soldiery. Our exertions and frustrations had made us bad-tempered and our various footslogging, pushing and paddling exercises had resulted in each of us receiving a thick coating of multi-coloured mud which, having started off by being just sticky, was now baked on us in hard and increasingly uncomfortable lumps. It was precisely at this moment that the officer commanding a flight of South African light bombers (I have no doubt he was a Major), decided that the opportunity for some convoy-strafing practice was too good to be missed. In turn, each of his aircraft dived at us from all angles, sweeping over us at a height of a few feet, before zooming up into the sky ready for the next run. Relief, however, was at hand in the shape of the Officer Commanding South Bound Convoy who had his car stranded on comparatively firm ground at the north end of the impassable section. We gratefully accepted his offer to take us on to Marsabit.

When a couple of weeks later Joy Percival left, we found ourselves not only literally holding the baby but passing her from one to the other with extreme caution. Infant hygiene was, of course, the order of the day and never were spoons and other utensils so conscientiously sterilised nor other basic anti-germ measures carried out with such care. Alison herself preferred to tackle the problem the other way around and to concentrate on developing her immunity system; in pursuance of which end she was on occasion found happily sharing a bone with the dog, suck for suck and lick for lick. Once she was discovered making a good meal out of a raw locust. As it turned out, only once during her first eighteen months of life did we have cause for any real concern. However, what our excellent Nursing Orderly had conscientiously and with good reason diagnosed to be an obviously serious bout of dysentery, turned out to be only a fondness for tomato juice. In our next station posting, we had a Medical Officer living next door and we constantly called on his services. It seems the availability of a doctor creates a great many illnesses, both real and imaginary.

(5)

A feature of the operational and post-operational war years in Marsabit was the number of air accidents which took place in the area. We frequently were called on to send out search and rescue parties, sometimes to specific points where a crash was known to have occurred and other times in the vague hope of gathering news of some aircraft reported as overdue, about which the only information was that it 'might possibly be in the Lake Rudolph region'. In a few cases, happily, rescues were made but more often all the occupants of the aircraft would be found dead or were missing and never traced. During the South African Army occupation, three crashes, including that of a rescue aircraft, occurred on the Didi Galgalla in a single day.

It was later, however, that we really became involved because Marsabit Mountain became a designated point in a standard training course flown by aircraft from a navigational school near Nairobi. The mist-covered mountain, combined with human error, was the direct cause of several tragic accidents while other accidents occurred in the vicinity as a result of mechanical failures. Our station handyman spent a remarkable amount of time knocking together coffins, a job at which he became an expert. We all became accustomed to performing gruesome tasks associated with air accidents, made the more gruesome by the fact that often we were forbidden to touch anything until the R.A.F. investigating party arrived. On one occasion, after everything had eventually been cleared and cleaned up, it was decided that the bodies should be taken down to Nanyuki. However, the necessary transport did not arrive until nearly midnight. I have never witnessed a more macabre scene: the five, rough coffins stacked outside the small guard-room near my office with the doubled sentries prowling round in the faint glimmer of a couple of storm lanterns, desperately trying to keep a pack of hyenas away, for this investigation had taken rather a long time.

Figure 42: (top) Marsabit: the District Commissioner's house, 1942, (bottom) view of the garden from the house. The large tree on the right was especially popular with the elephant.

Figure 43: (top) crashed aircraft on the Dida Galgalla, (bottom) Doreen and Bulgy.

Figure 44: (top) road up the Ethiopian escarpment on the way to Mega, (bottom) Boran stock at a waterhole in the foothills of Marsabit Mountain.

THE GLITTERING LAKE

On the 1ˢᵗ of February 1943, I had just arrived in my office in the early morning when the familiar moaning-sound of an aircraft came from the direction of the landing ground and I assumed it was about to land. Then there was a sudden silence and, as I shouted for the truck driver, there was a tremendous explosion. It turned out that this aircraft had been piloted by a young Belgian from Leopoldville in the Belgian Congo. He had been having engine trouble and had reported that he was going to land at Marsabit. Then one of his engines packed-up and he attempted to land on his remaining good engine. As he circled the landing ground, that second engine had failed - and the aircraft plummeted to the earth like a stone.

Contradictory messages caused confusion and it was the morning of the 3ʳᵈ before we could finally get down to clearing things up. We had, meanwhile, organised a work gang to do the best they could in the way of digging a common grave for the dead crew in the lava near the scene of the crash. An RAF padre had flown up with the crash investigating party and, at eleven in the morning, having done all we could, the burial service for the flight crew took place. Military honours were provided by a police bugler and a firing party. Doreen and Rosemary Whiteing brought wreaths made with flowers from their gardens and although these had come from only a few miles away, the fresh English flowers on the piles of black lava rocks put the final touch of incongruity to the scene: the white-cassocked padre, the white-robbed and turbaned Tribal Police, the gang of semi-naked Turkana road workers, the handful of prisoners from the gaol in white shorts and broad-arrowed shirts, leaning on their shovels; the two women in their bright dresses. The strong gale, whistling warm through the desolate thorn scrub and lava heaps, rattled the grotesque broken pieces of aircraft strewn all round us, including one complete wing that stood upright, huge and stark like some modern sculpture, providing a pre-arranged backcloth to the occasion. The pilot had been a Belgian and the crew came from England and three different Commonwealth countries. As always, in the face of the finality of death, man's pathetic futility shone out like a beacon; but in our remote corner, we had done our best to honour those men who had died while serving us, far from home.

That same afternoon, vigorous life took over from death, as was right and proper, putting a finishing touch to an unusual day. We had never been able to have Alison christened and the padre agreed that he was literally a heaven-borne, if not heaven-sent, opportunity. At ten months old, Alison, in her best and only party dress, took a close and lively interest in the proceedings which were conducted at one end of our small sitting-room. She had, of course, the advantage of being able to enjoy her own christening cake and made the most of this opportunity. So much and such mixed emotion left us limp and by the time we had seen the RAF party off, we felt we had had quite enough to keep us going for some time.

(6)

By June 1943, the Northern Frontier District was again in the front line, only this time the invader was the Desert Locust. That the threat would be serious had been foreseen for some time. It was the cause for very great concern, for the agricultural and pastoral lands of Kenya were, by now, important food-producing areas. Any major losses could seriously affect the general war effort.

Units of the Auxiliary Pioneer Corps were sent to Marsabit as the main striking force with local intelligence being made the responsibility of the Administration. The chief weapon relied on in this war was a poison bait, the basis of which was coffee husks and which locusts found extremely palatable. Other means of destruction were improvised to meet special situations as they arose.

In theory, the destruction of the Desert Locust was a simple matter. The eggs had been lying dormant in the ground throughout the long, dry season (or perhaps several years if they had been particularly dry ones) and had hatched out as soon

THE GLITTERING LAKE

as rain brought about the required conditions. The locusts first appeared as small hoppers whose immediate mobility was restricted to inches. However, after about ten days, they were large enough and strong enough to begin to band together in swarms and to move solidly in a generally southerly direction. After three weeks, they were full-grown and took to the air, their flights at first being short and wobbly. If, therefore, intelligence was sufficiently good and if transport, men and bait were adequate, it was merely a matter of getting the men and bait to the hopper bands within their period of vulnerability. In practice, however, even to locate the hopper bands over 26,000 square miles of country was a problem and much depended on the previous season's observations of mature swarms and consequent knowledge about their probable egg-laying areas; and all this depended on what degree of cooperation the Desert Locust Control organization had had from the people of half-a-dozen countries as locusts have no respect for international boundaries. If small, or large but comparatively compact, the locust bands could be dealt with quickly. Even if not totally destroyed, they could be so broken up and emasculated that the chances of their becoming a sizeable swarm in the flying stages were reduced to almost nil. During this 1943 campaign, it was found that most of the egg laying had taken place in a widely dispersed fashion, so that when the hoppers hatched out, they were far apart and spread out over huge areas. One hatching we located towards the south-west end of Lake Rudolph was estimated to cover more than 400 square miles, with an average of only about one hopper per square foot. In such circumstances, efficient destruction, with the means at our disposal, became almost impossible.

The Army did the job well, if with some natural distaste, for the men found it hard to accept such work as the kind of thing for which they had enlisted. Conditions were as tough and uncomfortable as in many a more exciting campaign. To have one's camp over-run by an enemy consisting of a strongly-moving band of hoppers was a very unpleasant experience. These hoppers just took over. To have thousands upon thousands of voracious grasshoppers piling into one's bed, food, clothes and hair was a form of misery which need hardly be experienced to be understood.

I stopped one morning for a mug of tea at a locust camp up the Moyale road where a very large Irish Sergeant was in charge. He had only recently arrived in the country and had been whisked off the ship and into the Auxiliary Pioneers almost immediately. I doubt he had ever seen an African before, let alone speak a word of any language which his men could understand; but he seemed to be getting on with the job. He found it difficult to exist on his rations as the form of packing made them much more suitable for several persons messing together. As he dismally opened an enormous tin of peas, he explained to me how he felt about things.

"I've got one brother in the Guards," he said, "and he has already got the Military Medal. I've another brother who's a Royal Marine commando and another who's a fighter pilot in the RAF. It's all very well but when the kids get bigger and start listening to their uncles' stories, they'll turn to me and say 'and what did you do in the war Daddy?' Well, all I'll be able to say is 'I fought bloody insects, m'dears!'"

(7)

By the middle of 1942, when the bulk of the Army had pulled out of Marsabit, the elephants began to return to the Mountain and re-stake their claim to their traditional haunts. These included our garden, where there was one tree near the house, which seemed to have some special appeal to them. After darkness had set in, we might hear the cracking and tearing of branches and a mighty rasping as one of them took a turn at scratching against the trunk. We would creep out and suddenly flash a torch on the tree. In an instant, the silence would be absolute and not an elephant to be seen anywhere. The way in which these great, lumbering creatures could melt away without a sound, the moment they found cause for alarm, was always a source of wonderment.

Later, the elephants became a greater nuisance and their nocturnal visits to our precious maize plantations round the station became so frequent that serious action against them reluctantly had to be taken, for it was a time of great food shortages. Assistant Inspector Mills of the Kenya Police, newly appointed to Marsabit, was appointed the official Elephant Control Officer as he was both a keen hunter and an accurate shot. He did not have to shoot many but he did gain the distinction of having shot two elephants during a pause in a game of bridge he was playing at our house one evening, a short time later: a feat perhaps for which he could have claimed some kind of world record. It was, at any rate, an aspect of the bridge game on which Mr Culbertson was found not to have given any clear guidance.

In general, it was not the elephant, buffalo or leopard in the surrounding forest which caused us any real trouble. The real troublemaker was that most revolting of God's creatures, the hyena. We seemed to specialise in a particularly large, daring and altogether nasty type. The traditional role of the animal, of course, was to slink about clearing up after lion had their fill of a kill; but like many other species, he has had to alter his habits to fit a changing environment. The hyena's idea of a manly life in his new Kenya environment has been mainly confined to such exercises as the shadowing of pregnant antelope and attacking them as they are giving birth; or when feeling particularly bold, breaking into cattle pens at night and having a quick meal off the softer parts of the crowded and terrified animals, leaving the most dreadful mutilations as evidence of the visit.

One of our favourite entertainments was to ride our ponies out into the desert in the afternoon and return late in the evening, or when the moon was full to ride back in the moonlight. One of our favourite rides was down the Moyale road and across the landing-strip. Often, we would find ourselves being escorted by a pack of ten or twelve hyenas on each side. Although they always kept a respectful distance, we speculated about what would happen if one was alone and had a serious fall. Hyenas are exceptionally powerful beasts for their size and when hungry are capable of devouring almost anything with their powerful jaws. Whilst I was stationed in Lodwar, a hyena one night dragged an extremely solid and heavy wooden bed through the narrow door of my cook's house, pulled it a few hundred yards and then ate to the last scrap the thick and ancient ox-hide strips which formed the 'springs' of the bed.

We experienced a lot of trouble in Marsabit with one particularly large and cunning animal. This hyena succeeded in demolishing heavy, wooden meat safes that stood on the back veranda of both our house and that of the police house and broke into our storerooms. We worked up a fiery hate for this animal after he demolished a heavy, wooden crate and ate a most delightful baby Grant's gazelle whose kennel the crate was. The gazelle had become a real pet to us and had kept us amused skidding across the polished concrete floors on his miniature hooves and curling up in front of the fire in our sitting room.

We made several unsuccessful attempts at eliminating this pestilential creature. Eventually, Pat and Rosemary decided to mount a serious and carefully planned operation. Their police house was a minute, wooden bungalow, indeed just a very large box with a corrugated iron lid. At one end of the back veranda was a small storeroom in which all the household and edible stores were kept; an identical structure at the other end acted as Pat's dressing room. Their plan was simple. A suitable bait would be placed on the veranda at night, a lamp would be left alight in the living room, sited in such a way that a faint glimmer would be thrown on the back veranda through the half open door, hopefully just sufficient to ensure visibility without scaring off the hyena. Pat, ensconced in his dressing room, would shoot the animal through his dressing room door. To this end, he spent an afternoon cutting a porthole in the door through which to shoot. As a precaution, the storeroom opposite was to be emptied of all valuables, edible or otherwise, in case of damage from a stray shot or a rampaging hyena.

Following a lull in his nocturnal activities, the hyena again visited our house one night; we decided that as the following night would probably be the turn of Pat and Rosemary's house, all arrangements to spring the trap should be made. A stinking lump of goat's meat was tied securely to a stout table on the back veranda. Rosemary removed all her crockery and other valuables from the store, including most importantly Pat's recently arrived ration of beer – a whole new case of bottles which at the time was such an unusual object that just looking at it gave him exquisite pleasure. These treasures were carefully stacked on the table in the living room. The lamp was accurately sited, the door suitably adjusted; a shotgun loaded with S.S.G., together with a torch, was placed in readiness.

We had supper with Pat and Rosemary that evening to celebrate the occasion and they went to bed just after we left. The light was still burning in their bedroom when they heard a shuffling noise outside. They waited for a few moments then crept to the door to look out on to the back veranda. Whilst they could still hear strange noises, they could see no sign of their visitor. They then realised with a shock that the sounds were coming from inside the house. Treading stealthily, they peeped through the doorway leading into the living room, Pat in front and Rosemary just behind ready to shine the torch over his shoulder. There, under the dining room table and chewing his bone in a most domesticated fashion, squatted a huge, stinking hyena. If Pat fired and missed, or only wounded the animal, he would be landed in a most difficult situation, with a dangerous customer at close and in very cramped quarters. Moreover, he might upset the table on which rested the precious beer and crockery. However, it was no time for such idle speculation and Pat fired his shotgun. It was a difficult angle and he scored a direct hit on the case of beer with a couple of stray 'outers' on two of his wife's best tea cups. The hyena bellowed, lurched from under the table and went to ground behind the sofa. Pat quickly followed it there and despatched the hyena with his next shot. We had a rest from hyenas; but it was days before Rosemary could remove the mixture of blood and beer off her carpets, walls and furniture. And the filthy stench of hyena clung to the house for a long time.

(8)

Not long after Doreen had arrived in Marsabit, a squadron of South African armoured cars passed through from Ethiopia on their way south. Whilst travelling through the village of Alghe, some distance to the north of Mega, the commander of the last car in the convoy noticed a white fox-terrier loping along behind them. He stopped and helped her into the car, for it turned out to be a very pregnant 'her'. A few days, later she produced a litter of six puppies. These the commander was now trying to dispose of - and we were given the first pick.

It was in this way that Bulgy came into our lives, a very respectable-looking if somewhat robust, smooth-haired fox-terrier. His name was nothing to do with his appearance, although he did grow up to suit it. It was, in a flash of inspiration, derived from that childhood jingle:

'Algy went for a walk;

He met a bear;

The bear was bulgy,

The bulge was Algy.'

Fundamentally, there was nothing wrong with Bulgy; it was just that he was an irrepressible extrovert. It may be that the unique distinction of being born in an armoured car went to his head; or possibly that this first week's spoiling by the soldiers fixed in his mind the single idea on which his whole future way of life and personal outlook was based. For Bulgy firmly believed he was the most popular dog in the world and no amount of scolding, walloping or disciplining in any shape or form ever got this idea out of his mind. If he had just thought that we ourselves loved him through good and ill (which, on the whole, we did) all would have been well. However, he was utterly convinced that everyone, no matter what colour, creed, caste, class, age and occupation not only loved him above all other creatures but was longing to tell him that he was the most wonderful dog that ever roamed this earth.

We survived Bulgy's earlier attempts to woo the local population, both civil and military, by appealing to his various victims' good nature. Pride of ownership palled, our smiles became more and more sickly and the expression 'he's only a puppy' became less and less convincing. Bulgy had, of course, a high social position as the District Commissioner's dog. Moslems learned to tolerate his attentions, I think possibly after re-reading the Koran with more care or by working out some special form of dispensation. A letter of abject apology usually sufficed with the higher service ranks and other senior Christians. The local pagans thought we were mad anyway and they decided to accept Bulgy's overtures as just another interesting manifestation of this fact.

Bulgy's special method of showing and seeking affection was to jump up. Not just a normal doggy jump - but one into which he put his whole being, mind and spirit. He achieved a degree of skill and height at this infuriating pastime that I have never, before or since, seen equalled. In the Dog Olympics, he would have achieved the Gold Medal for the 'jumping up' contest. We tried beating him and cajoling him, we tried standing on his toes; we tried all the other training tricks glibly put forward by the experts in any book we could find. The experts, of course, had never met Bulgy. In time, you can get used to anything and having given up in despair, we just let matters take their course.

It may have been that the idea of new fields to conquer, new friends to make and the heady attraction of superior rank encouraged Bulgy to an excess of zeal. Whatever it was, he scored his first major triumph with a new Commissioner of Police who was paying his first official visit of inspection to Marsabit. It was a wet, misty day with the Marsabit mud at its stickiest. Bulgy did not even give the Commissioner time to get out of his car. It was a brand-new, shining, dark blue car, one of a new fleet which was the pride and glory of the Police Force. This well-polished car had not drawn to a standstill before Bulgy was trying to scramble in a window, with mud flying in all directions and back claws scoring a myriad of deep scars down the side of the glossy door. We hauled him off and the Commissioner really took it quite well. We promised Pat faithfully that we would tie Bulgy up the next day.

We did tie him up; but it took more than a piece of rope to keep Bulgy away from his new-found friend. It was another wet morning, although the low clouds had cleared by the time the official parade was due to start. The Commissioner, wearing a spotless and carefully pressed uniform, had just finished his inspection of the police guard-of-honour. He was preparing to address the assembled troops when Bulgy arrived; it was the end of a two-hundred-yard sprint down our very muddy driveway. He never even hesitated a moment, there was no change in pace, Bulgy was straight on target first shot, a fine tribute to his powers of recognition. He managed at least three high, muddy jumps before the horror-struck police sprang into action. Five of them rushed forward, getting in each other's way in their eagerness to be the one to catch hold of the offending animal. Bulgy was taken away, still kicking and struggling. The orange-red splashes of mud, lumps and smears really made quite attractive patterns on the new uniform.

Through experience, we became much better at locking-up Bulgy. However, a long while afterwards we had the Governor of Kenya, the late Sir Henry Moore and Lady Moore, staying with us for a few days. Naturally, we kept Bulgy well-away and, I'm sure to his great disappointment, hardly met the distinguished visitors. Nevertheless, his instinct did not fail him. We had been out all day and before evening dinner, the Governor was relaxing in a chair reading a book by the fire. Somehow, Bulgy appeared at the door, took a sniff and a quick look round. Before I could make a move, he dashed in and with a mighty leap landed in the lap of a very startled Sir Henry. Fortunately, for both Bulgy and me, the Governor was fond of dogs.

Bulgy's bumptiousness was once nearly the cause of tragedy. I was away on safari and Tom Askwith, the District Commissioner, Isiolo, and his wife, Pat, were spending the night with Doreen. As was our usual way of entertaining visitors, she took them for a walk up to Sokorte Dikka in the late afternoon to view any game which might have come down for their evening drink. This was normally a safe enough pastime, provided one took standard precautions. Bulgy joined the party, of course, notwithstanding the fact that he had been firmly left at home. As there seemed to be nothing much happening and it was a long way to take him back, they decided to let him come with them.

On the way home, in the failing light, there was a great crash in front of the group and an elephant lumbered out of the forest and across the pathway. They gave him time to get out of the way, Doreen having grabbed hold of Bulgy firmly. When all seemed clear, they hurried on, but Bulgy, breaking loose, dived into the trees and started dashing about barking furiously. An elephant appeared in front of them and glancing behind, they saw another; then more elephants materialised amongst the trees on both sides of the path and immediately they realised they were right in the middle of a sizeable herd. One thing you must not do is to take a dog near an elephant because it will dash at the animal, barking and then run back to you for protection, probably with the elephant in pursuit. Bulgy was now giving a perfect demonstration of the soundness of this rule. The party returned to the house safely after a very frightening experience, thankful that the Marsabit elephants had maintained their reputation for mildness.

Poor Bulgy: we could cope with him in Marsabit but when, later on, we took him down-country to a more thickly inhabited and civilized station, life became impossible. Bulgy had to go; but I have no doubt that he parted from this life in peace; and still holding firmly to the comfortable belief that he was the most popular dog in the world, as perhaps he is in the next.

(9)

It was the thing which the people of Marsabit liked least about the war which seemed likely would bring them the greatest long-term benefits – the sale of cattle. This was a matter of special concern as regards the Boran who bred splendid animals on the Mountain and whose main source of wealth they were. Indeed, these beasts were the foundation stock of the East African Boran breed of cattle. But it applied also to the Rendille and Gabbra, notwithstanding the fact their riches lay mainly in their vast herds of camels. All three tribes also owned huge numbers of sheep and goats.

Before the War, a steady trade had gone on in sheep and goats with itinerant Somali stock traders buying them in ones and twos all over the District and then taking them out through Isiolo when a sufficiently large herd had been amassed. There was, however, no export trade in cattle, for their movement from the Northern Frontier District into other parts of Kenya was strictly prohibited. There was a very real danger of spreading diseases, on the control of which great effort had been expended but not the huge effort and expense which would have been required to bring the whole of the country within the control system. It was not a matter to which either the Boran or the other tribes objected for to them, as to all cattle-owning tribes, the question of selling cattle was something which just did not arise. Had some well-meaning person come along and arranged a mass meeting to inform the Boran that they were being discriminated against in this matter of stock movement, they would have listened politely and then asked him what in the world he was talking about. Cattle were things to amass, to exchange for wives, to compensate for wrongs, to hand on to one's heirs and finally, importantly, to admire. For was it not a man's dream that, as he grew into old age and the pleasures of contemplation replaced the vigorous passions of youth, he would have the great joy of watching daily his multiplying herds and have the intense satisfaction which only the sight, sound and feel of cattle – his cattle – could provide? The sale of cattle was an idea as alien to the cattle tribesman as the outright sale of land was to his agricultural counterpart. That was the tradition. It had broken down to some small extent through the internal sale to township butchers of small numbers to meet local needs; but this was regarded more as a magnanimous gesture to assist the Government than as a normal commercial transaction. Cattle were your life, your being, your hope on earth and hereafter. They were things you wanted; of what possible value would it be to exchange them for shillings, which you did not want, or wanted very few of? A few were needed to pay your tax, to buy a piece of cloth, some sugar, a knife, perhaps a roll of wire a wife had an eye on. However, if you could at all help it, you just did not dispose of your real wealth for such trivial purposes. Because traditionally there was no market for cattle and because no one thought of them in monetary terms, they had no value in our sense of the word. Fifteen to twenty-five shillings was the price for slaughter stock; the price for cows never arose. If an outsider living in the district wanted to keep cows for milk, he hired them at some agreed value for the lactation period.

In the desert areas, a fair balance was maintained between grazing and livestock. There were no veterinary services and the country was, by nature, so environmentally severe that nothing could make it worse. When grazing and water ran out, large numbers of stock of all kinds died and that was the end of it. The problem on the Mountain was of a different nature. Here there was wonderful grazing available and, year by year as the Boran herds increased, the problem of overstocking increased also. As always happens in such circumstances, and in common with all the main pastoral areas in Kenya (and indeed of Africa), the result was a steady deterioration in the quality of the stock and in the quality and quantity of the grazing areas. The loss in wealth was appalling. However, the solid arguments for stock control which were just beginning to have some impact on the minds of certain other pastoral tribes who were surrounded by and gradually acquiring a taste for the joys and benefits of civilization, literally meant nothing to the Boran. Turn your surplus cattle into hard cash and you will become rich with the many things money can buy; you can have education for your children, better health services, good roads; and you can improve your water supplies and grazing, establish veterinary services and so make many times more valuable the reduced number of cattle which your land can safely carry. These were the general cries of the Administration; to the Boran, they had no bearing even on the fringe of reality.

The only positive contribution to the war effort required of the Marsabit tribes was the selling of livestock to provide rations for the troops stationed in the immediate neighbourhood early in the war and as a contribution to the general Kenya Colony pool later on.

To say that the tribes made their contribution with great reluctance is but to state the truth. However, when one considers how alien was the whole idea and how small their understanding of the issues about which the War was being fought, their cooperation was excellent. Indeed, throughout the period of the War, they never seriously failed with their quotas. Whatever their own immediate views, this compulsory sale of livestock was the best thing that could have happened from any long-term outlook. Not only did it provide some quick relief to the hard-pressed grazing areas and skimmed off the low-quality cattle - but it had the effect of breaking down what had been the previously insurmountable barrier to cattle export. Precautions were taken to prevent the spread of disease: by inoculation and through the establishment of special holding areas in suitable parts of Kenya and by ensuring the cattle reached the butcher as quickly as possible; but risks were accepted which would never have been in a time of peace. An outlet was for the first time established and as the tribesmen began to accumulate money so they gradually began to have some realisation of what this financial wealth could buy for them. To begin with, the very top price for the best slaughter stock was the unprecedented amount of £2; by 1943, prices had moved steadily upwards and high-quality animals fetched £15-20.

Initially, when the demand was relatively low, I used to

buy the cattle myself but as the War machine requirements increased, buying was taken over by a succession of military and quasi-military units until finally it was absorbed into the Colony-wide Livestock Control Organisation. One of the earliest outfits which suddenly arrived in Marsabit and assumed buying responsibility, was a section of what was then called the K.C.C.C. standing, I believe, for the Kenya Cattle Collecting Company or some similar mouthful. A senior Government Veterinary officer had been put in charge of it with the rank of Lieutenant-Colonel, with several junior members of the Veterinary Department serving under him. This Veterinary officer was a well-known character and was widely reputed to be the meanest man in Kenya. On their first visit, his two companions in the vehicle had a bet as to which of them could trick him into smoking one of his own cigarettes between Isiolo and Marsabit but he confounded all their stratagems.

The institution of cattle sales had a positive social as well as an economic effect. The nomadic pastoral tribes of the Northern frontier had no recognised meeting places for social exchanges, unlike the regular markets which are such a feature of settled African communities. The nearest approach was the gathering together to water livestock at the wells and waterholes but there was usually too much work to be done to make possible anything other than a swift exchange of gossip. As soon as the sales grudgingly became accepted, they quickly developed into social occasions of comparative gaiety. Other minor trading occurred on the fringes and women and girls would turn up in substantial numbers and in their best finery. The women were not as worried as the men about parting with the family cattle. They quickly and joyously converted as many jingling shillings as they could prise from their menfolk into cloth and trinkets from the hovering merchants. Unfortunately, trade goods of all kinds were for a long time in very short supply and so the part they could play in popularising the livestock sales was limited accordingly. Harry Benson became our regular buyer on behalf of the Livestock Control Organisation and when he eventually moved on to another area, the local people found it difficult to get used to the new man. They had come to trust Harry's valuations of their stock. There was also the additional advantage that, when Harry announced the price he would pay, there was no doubt what that price was; for no combination of wind, shouting herdsmen and bellowing cattle could defeat him. Any arguments he might have were public and for all to hear, even if not everyone could completely understand his fluent mixture of Swahili, Boran and Australian.

(10)

One of the District's great eccentrics was Tomal Kopess, an ex-Rendille Government Headman whose cheerful insanity increased with his years. He was a very wealthy man with a most respected position in the tribe. He sincerely felt that his counterpart in the British hierarchy was the Sovereign: every few months, loud noises-off would indicate that Kopess was paying his 'state visit' to Marsabit. The old man would burst into my office, emanating good cheer, good fellowship and good intentions. Discarding a variety of sticks, stools and possibly a spear or two on the veranda behind him as he clambered over the sill of the window entrance (no one ever used the doorway), he would advance towards me, bellowing his greetings.

"Hello, hello, hello, District Commissioner. Kopess is here! Kopess has come! Kopess has left his beautiful camels to come and visit you! Are you well?"

"Good morning, Kopess. I'm glad to see you! Are you well? Where have you come from?"

"Kopess is well and when Kopess is well, the world is well. I have come from Sirima where the countryside is white with Kopess's camels. And tell me now, how is the King in London? He got my last message, yes? Kopess and the King George are one and if Kopess is well, then the King sleeps quietly. And when are you coming to see me? I have been keeping an especially fat young camel to slaughter in your honour......"

And so on, for over half an hour. The 'especially fat, young camel' was a feature of all Kopess's personal greetings to me and unless it had been renewed on occasions, it must have been getting a little tough by the time I had eventually got around to accepting his long-standing invitation.

It was during the rainy season and Kopess's people were camped at the western edge of the Hedad. After a period of noisy greetings, he shouted to a man nearby who immediately dived into a mud hut, to emerge a few moments later carrying a large greater kudo horn on which he proceeded to blow a prolonged fanfare. Only a few people were present to witness the occasion as nearly all the adults were out tending the livestock or performing various essential chores such as collecting firewood and drawing water. He expressed regret that it was not the evening when I could have seen and admired his vast milk herds as they were brought into camp. He then conducted me into his dwelling, the cool, clean and tidy interior of which was in marked contrast to its exterior. From the outside, it appeared like little more than a pile of smelly and very dirty animal hides thrown over a framework of sticks. Bowls of fresh camel's milk were produced and passed around those who were present. To my great regret, as on other similar occasions, I was unable to stomach more than a token sip: with regret because camel's milk is highly nutritious and was regularly quaffed with evident enjoyment by several of my colleagues; and also because it seemed discourteous not to drain the bowl. I could hardly stomach cow's milk even from the cleanest and clearest of crystal goblets and this ordinary dislike of milk, combined with the knowledge that the local drinking vessels were customarily scoured with cow's or camel's urine was always too much for me.

The opportunity was taken to introduce me to the oldest, living Rendille whose age was judged to be one hundred and eight years. This was a great age anywhere in the world but one which was almost unheard of amongst these hard-living, quick-dying nomads. A very wizened and frail old man was curled up under a shelter. A young girl squatted beside him, fanning him with a bunch of leaves to keep the flies moving. On being spoken to, he stirred and looked up. After some explanation of what was required, he gave a toothless grin and whipped off his loincloth to display a great scar in his side which he said he received from a Gabbra spear when he was a young man. After a few minutes of rather desultory conversation during which the old man re-fought in mime this particular fight and explained in detail how he had disposed of his Gabbra opponent, he suddenly sat up straight and stared at me with his bleary, old eyes.

"Are you the Government?" he demanded.

"Well, sort of," I cautiously replied.

He gave a chuckle that seemed to come from somewhere deep down in his wrinkled stomach.

"Well, yes; yes, you could say that I am the Government," I concluded, having tried to condense into a few simple and well chosen phrases the history and tradition of the British colonial system, the Kenya constitution and the manner in which the Provincial Administration fitted into the picture.

"Oh – so you're the Government, are you? Well, young man, do you know when I last saw the Government?"

"No," I confessed as he continued to chuckle and gurgle, "I can't even begin to guess."

"Young man, Aw-cha was the last Government I saw."

Not being at that time very well versed in my East African history, this name rang no immediate bell. All I could do was express polite surprise and even astonishment. On my return to Marsabit, I quickly identified that the grizzled old man's last official contact with the Government as Mr G.F. Archer who was one of East Africa's best known early administrators. This meeting must have taken place in the first decade of the 20th Century. Archer constructed the first building ever erected in Marsabit. It was beside Sokorte Guda and it was from its ruins that the Martin Johnston's obtained stones for the house they built nearby. I felt that my attempts at close administration were not as brilliant as I had fondly imagined.

No one had mentioned anything about the 'especially fat, young camel.'

(11)

On the 8th September 1943, at 8.30 p.m., Mohamed Said, the excellent Assistant District Clerk, an Arab from the Coast province, burst into our sitting room beside himself with excitement. He announced he had just picked up the news of Italy's capitulation on his wireless. The last time Mohamed Said had been involved in any excitement had been the previous Christmas Eve. With great difficulty, we had rescued him from a very drunken District Clerk, his immediate superior who in the middle of the night had set out with the absurd alcoholic impression that Mohamed had stolen his watch during a game of cards earlier in the evening.

On hearing the announcement of Italy's capitulation, Jack Carter who was then the Assistant Superintendent of Police, set to work immediately. By 9.45 p.m., we had mustered on the lawn in front of my office the entire force of Kenya Police, Tribal Police, Prison warders and anyone else who could legitimately produce a firearm. After I had announced the good news to the assembled throng and had called for three cheers in the good British tradition, we fired a *feu de joie* with live ammunition. The volleys were a little ragged and were punctuated by some rapid bursts from Sten guns and a few mighty explosions from a sporting rifle. As the night was extremely dark, the operation was almost as impressive as it was dangerous. Years later, I learned that all this jollification had not escaped the retribution which followed inexorably any attempt to brighten life at His Majesty's expense; a shocked Audit Department in Nairobi (no Auditor had, to my knowledge, ever penetrated as far as Marsabit since the station was first opened) had quite properly called attention to the extraordinary figures in the September monthly ammunition return and enquired whether it really had been profitable to squeeze so much musketry practice into one day.

A few days later, we heard that I was to be transferred to the Kikuyu district of Fort Hall. We fixed on 8th October for our departure. John Dowson was to take over from me and consignments of his heavy baggage and household goods had already begun to arrive. The baggage on one of the first trucks included some twenty-four ducks and chickens, which, as it turned out, the Dowson's were never to see again.

Doreen had always been a keen poultry keeper. No matter where we have been stationed, she always managed to produce our own eggs, the eating of which, with great enjoyment, has usually been my sole contribution to this allegedly joint enterprise. She had, however, at this particular time, and after many months of earnest entreaty, succeeded in making me realise that the very least I could do would be to organise the station carpenter to make her a decent animal-proof chicken-run; for every imaginable type of predator from leopard to mongoose had only to slink out of the forest nearby for a few minutes to obtain a fine chicken supper. We decided that this chicken-run would be a very special one, a permanent structure capable of withstanding the assault of almost anything smaller than elephant or rhino. We also knew we could make it at little cost out of forest-timber off-cuts, large quantities of which were lying scattered round the site of an ex-military sawmill.

The carpenter reduced these off-cuts to about eight feet in length. These were then stood side by side in a narrow trench some eighteen inches in depth. The trench was then filled in and the earth rammed down tightly. By adding some cross pieces and the occasional large nail to hold the less regular lengths together, a very stout palisade resulted. To me, it appeared very much like an illustration from the adventures of 'Masterman Ready', except that it was not under attack by spear-waving cannibals. A strong door was made on one side and a henhouse was built in one corner, with a door of its own so that the birds could be doubly locked up at night. The whole rectangular palisade was then roofed over with wire netting to keep out the hawks. Without this netting, these birds of prey would have had no trouble in swooping down and carrying off in their talons our prized chickens.

We were very proud of this chicken-run and Doreen was delighted with it. So, it was a real blow when we heard that we were being transferred, just as the final touches had been made. However, this had been, and was to continue to be, the fate of many of our more enterprising efforts. This new chicken-run did, at least, solve the problem of the Dowson farmyard which had suddenly, without prior notice, descended on us as there was plenty of room for all. We shoved the lot inside, with feelings of relief that they were not going to be a troublesome responsibility.

A couple of nights later, Doreen woke me up at about 2 a.m. to say that she had heard noises from the direction of the chicken-run and hadn't I better go and see what was happening? After some scathing remarks about the forest always being full of strange noises and the delivery of a short lecture on wives who kept on hearing things, reluctantly I sallied forth armed with a torch and a stout walking stick. The chicken-run was wrapped in silence and a cursory inspection of the perimeter walls revealed no breach in the defences. Muttering Part 2 of the wives' lecture, I hurried back indoors.

"Any sign of anything?" Doreen queried sleepily, without bothering so much as to raise her head from the pillow or even to open her eyes.

"No, of course not," I replied with masculine assurance and added: "I've never known anyone like you for 'hearing things'. If there had been anything of significance, I would have heard it also. Now go back to sleep, the trouble with you is that you can never distinguish dreams from reality."

The next morning, we visited the chicken-run. The majority of chickens and ducks were as sprightly as ever and they paid no attention to the thirteen slain corpses stretched out on the floor of the hen-house: ten of ours and three of the Dowson's. I avoided Doreen's glaring eyes. What I had missed that night was now plain to see. Something quite large had tunnelled under the door of the palisade and then under the door of the hen-house. To her credit, Doreen refrained from repeating 'I told you so' more than a couple of times but I could see it in her eyes as we filled in the tunnels with large stones and dug more in under the door to make further tunnelling impossible. A conference of all the most knowledgeable people in the station concluded that the night raider had been a honey-badger – an animal I did not then know existed in Africa, let alone in Marsabit.

Two nights later, we both heard a noise but this time I was prepared and rushed out with a gun and torch. Something carrying a hen went streaking past me into a clump of bushes where a great commotion started. I fired off both barrels into the middle of the bushes. I scored a bull's eye on Doreen's champion-laying Rhode Island Red but failed to shoot the badger. This time, the creature had tunnelled under the foundations of the palisade which under different circumstances would have deserved a great deal of admiration. I must have arrived shortly after he had completed his mining operation because there were no corpses in the hen-house; and although the ducks were huddled into a heap at one corner, the chickens were sitting quietly on their perches, cocking their heads to one side to peer at me with beady eyes. Once again, we filled in the tunnels and went back to bed, confident that if I had done nothing else, I must have at least given the badger a nasty shock and possibly even a headache.

We soon discovered that our confidence was misplaced and our assessment of a honey-badger's tenacity grossly underestimated. Next morning, we found another tunnel and the sickening remains of another mighty slaughter. Only nine birds remained alive out of the joint Thorp-Dowson flock. This time, we left the tunnel as it was and concealed a wicked-looking leopard trap on the inside. It was sprung that night and, although the badger was not caught, he must have been frightened away as none of the remaining birds had been harmed. We re-set the trap and hid it more cunningly. It was sprung again and, somewhat mystified, we recovered lumps of fine grey fur from its jaws. This proved to belong to Jack Carter's beloved grey Persian cat who, although somewhat shaken after her miraculous escape and slightly shorn, was otherwise none the worse for her nocturnal adventure.

The following day, I set off for a final safari to the north to bid farewell to the various Police posts and to such tribal elders as I could find. I spent the first night at North Horr. This post was now very modern and boasted a wireless set which worked spasmodically. As I was having breakfast next morning, a signaller came in and solemnly handed me a message. The message was from Jack Carter and it read:

"BITER BIT BADGER BUMPED STOP HOW MANY SHAVING BRUSHES QUERY"

(12)

I have noticed that it is necessary only to fix a date to depart from somewhere for everything to start happening all at once. Indeed, time itself suddenly begins folding up like a dropped accordion. From having all the time in the world to do a limited number of jobs, you quickly find you have an unlimited number to do in no time at all.

With the badger having single-handedly disposed of our poultry, at least one packing problem was solved; and, when I returned from my final safari, we decided we must really get down to sorting out our belongings and prepare ourselves physically and mentally to leave. It was just at this point that Sub-Area Headquarters requested urgent help to remove what was left of their salvage dump some miles outside of Marsabit; two Italian prisoners-of-war (a mason and a carpenter) whom I had indented for a long time ago to help build a new hospital, were delivered to me without warning; the Boran decided it was an appropriate moment to begin a new elephant-killing campaign in the forest; in return, the elephant, unconcerned about distinguishing friend from foe, launched an attack of unprecedented ferocity on the spring-head installations of our water-supply – which they had been allowing us to enjoy in peace for ages; all the long-awaited materials for a township maize-mill arrived; the Tax Clerk went on strike, had a flaming row with Mohamed Said and had to be instantly dismissed; an outbreak of rinderpest, a serious cattle disease, was reported in one Gabbra herd; the District Commissioner, Rumuruti, complained that large numbers of Rendille were illegally crossing the Marsabit boundary; Gerald Reece complained at insufficient progress on the Buluk-Bani Road; the Italian prisoners complained about their rations; the festival of Id-Ul-Fitr suddenly happened with the new moon and the local Moslems wanted to make a special show of it because the Italians were no longer our enemies; an Assistant Agricultural Officer whom I had been trying to recruit for two years turned up from Garissa. I no longer know why but nine days before our departure I myself decided the time was appropriate to do a job I had been contemplating for a very long time: to re-thatch the main building of our house. The roof had been leaking badly and I suppose I thought it would be a friendly gesture to have a new roof in place before the arrival of the Dowson's. We stripped the old thatch off in no time and possibly everything would have been all right had the station foreman informed me a little sooner that there was a shortage of thatching grass. We soon discovered that what had been cut and stacked was not nearly enough for our purposes. John Dowson arrived on the 4th October; to his great credit, he took both his roofless home and a most chaotic handing-over very well.

We pulled out of Marsabit at 8.30 a.m. on the 8th October in a flurry of farewells and without time to think of the awful finality of the moment - for although we felt it was time for a change, we loved Marsabit dearly. It was most unlikely that we would ever see it or any of our many friends there again – nor have we. The Northern Frontier District said its own farewell to us before we crossed its boundary at Isiolo. First, the exhaust pipe fell of the truck; then the fan cut the radiator overflow pipe; and, finally, we experienced our very last N.F.D. puncture.

It was our daughter Alison who had the last word. Having lived her first eighteen months in an almost wholly male society, it took her some ten days before she would tolerate any woman other than her mother. Friends, aunts, cousins, even doting grandmother were all the same to her and she would scream her head off as soon as one came within her vision. However, she learned to walk during the two days we spent on a farm at 9,000 feet above sea level on the way down to Nairobi. If in this other way she was a little odd for a while after her time in Marsabit, it was probably just an unconscious determination to keep in step with her parents.

APPENDIX

THE GELUBBA OF THE OMO DELTA

A note on the tribe and its external relations, 1888 – 1943

(1)

INTRODUCTION

The Omo (called the Nianam in some of the earlier records) is a sizeable river and the only permanent watercourse flowing into Lake Rudolf. Its high rainfall catchment area in the southwestern highlands of Ethiopia is an extensive one; in the wet seasons tremendous floods are poured into the north end of the Lake whose waters become discoloured for many miles. A number of small tribes live in the delta area, one of which is the Gelubba – referred to by sundry early writers as the Reshiat, the Goliba, the Ghelab or the Gheleba. They have also been called the Rusia although this term was more usually used to designate their country. In the Turkana District on the western shore of Lake Rudolf, the tribe has always been known as the Merille, possibly having been confused in earlier times with the Murle.

Since the early days of British Administration on the southwestern border of Ethiopia, the Gelubba have gained considerable notoriety; although on occasion they have undoubtedly been credited (or more correctly debited) with various misdeeds which may well have been performed by some of their various neighbours. They have been a permanent headache to generations of Kenya administrative officers; for living as they do with a foot in three territories, Kenya, the Sudan and Ethiopia (and in the most inaccessible corner of each), the Gelubba have been ideally placed for the flouting of all authority from whatever source or direction. When infrequently they have reached the headlines of the newspapers, it has been in connection with large-scale raiding operations into Kenya or with the holding of some international border conference concerning compensation for murder and looting perpetrated during earlier forays. The victims of their unwelcome attentions have usually been one of the four nearest Kenya tribes, namely, the Gabbra, the Rendille, the Turkana and the Samburu (earlier writers have referred to the Turkana as the Elgume and the Samburu as the Lokob). Gelubba raiding parties, however, have not always had it all their own way.

Until it became an operational area early in the 1939 – 1945 war, the northern Lake Rudolf region was a veritable *terra incognita* as far as Europeans were concerned; and was known only to a handful of administrative, army and police officers, to a few travellers and to members of a very few scientific expeditions which had penetrated the area. For a period in 1941, army units on both sides of the delta lived amongst the Gelubba; and during the previous three years they had nominally been under Italian administration. The Gelubba's only other serious contact with Europeans had been with Count Teleki's party, during his exploratory wanderings in 1888.

Protection of British tribesmen from Gelubba raids had been a major task of the Kenya administration in the area from the earliest days; and into this negative form of occupation had to be channelled the greater part of such resources as were available, to the detriment of more positive and progressive activities. Up to 1940, notwithstanding many high-sounding phrases and the enunciation of lofty moral principles, neither their Ethiopian nor subsequent Italian overlords had been able to make the Gelubba pay anything substantial in the way of compensation for the losses inflicted on the Turkana, Rendille, Gabra and Samburu over a long period. Border meetings were held at infrequent intervals in attempts to settle outstanding claims and grievances. While these usually created a temporary climate of goodwill and sometimes resulted in the production of a paper settlement of some kind, the practical results were usually extremely disappointing. The closing ceremony of one such meeting, held in 1934, was described briefly as follows:

'The ratification of the peace necessitated the killing of a white sheep and a white bull, both supplied by the elders of the aggressor tribe. It was interesting to note that although the Chief of the Turkana was present, he took no part in the actual ceremony as he was still a warrior and therefore led them in battle only. The elders of either tribe squatted in a row, all the Turkana being in this case on the left and the Merille on the right. The white sheep was then killed in front of the assembled elders. Strings of fat were taken from the entrails and draped round the necks of the Turkana by the elders of the Merille. The white bull was then slaughtered, a bone from the front leg broken with a stone and the marrow sucked from a half by the chief elder of the two tribes. This completed the ceremony and all concerned sat down to feast on the carcasses of the two beasts.'[9]

In more recent times, the Rendille, living well south of the border, had enjoyed a long and welcome respite from Gelubba attentions. It was therefore something of a shock to read in the newspapers in January 1952 that they had been subjected to a serious attack; the Gelubba raiding party slaughtering twenty women, five men and forty-nine children. A feature of Gelubba raiding has been their pre-occupation with killing as opposed to the more usual border habit of concentrating on loot; loot to the Gelubba always seems to have been of secondary importance. There has been at least one raid on record when the raiders slaughtered captured stock when they found no hope of getting it away. In April 1952, the Kenya Police brought a Gelubba party to action and were obliged to use automatic weapons against heavy rifle fire in a seven-hour battle. The following notes, however, deal only with events up to 1943. Save where otherwise stated, the facts recorded have been taken from sundry unpublished documents which formed part of the Political Records of the Marsabit District.

(2)
TRAVELLERS' ACCOUNTS OF THE GELUBBA, 1888-1943
Teleki and Von Hohnel 1888

On the 14 April 1888, Count Samuel Teleki met the Gelubba in their villages at the northern end of Lake Rudolf and, as far as is known, this was their first contact with Europeans. Von Hohnel described in some detail their dealings with them.[10] The tribe was then in a very flourishing condition.

Donaldson-Smith 1894-1895[11]

Seven years later, in 1894-1895, two travellers arrived in the area almost at the same time. Dr Donaldson-Smith (in 'Unknown African Countries') reports on the Gelubba as follows: 'The Reshiat were not in the same thriving condition as they were when discovered by Count Teleki. All their cattle had been carried away by disease and the Abore[12] had stolen most of their donkeys .... now there is scarcely anything left of this once rich and powerful tribe. There are not more than 500 inhabitants in Rusia and these can scarcely keep body and soul together on the little durrha (millet) that they can raise. Many of them have been obliged to resort to fishing as a means of earning their living; and still greater numbers have crossed the River Nianam and settled in Rusia villages on the north-west corner of Lake Rudolf, in the country of Elgume.'[13]

Neumann, 1894-1895

Neumann (in 'Elephant Hunting in East Equatorial Africa') states that he found the Reshiat a satisfactory people to deal with and that he had 'pictured a populous and extensive district' to find only a few villages scattered along the Lake shore. He later learned that more Reshiat lived north-west of the Lake.

Vittorio Bottego, 1896

In 1896, Vittorio Bottego found that the Omo and Nianam were one and the same river. He found the Gelubba living in the delta of the Omo and in the marshy north-west corner of the lake. The higher ground further west he found, surprisingly, inhabited by Rendille.

Cavendish and Andrew, 1897

In March 1897, H.S.H. Cavendish and H. Andrew arrived at the north end of Lake Rudolf. Cavendish states that the Gelubba 'were now literally starving, having been looted by the Boran on several occasions and having lost all their wealth of cattle through rinderpest.'

Austin, 1898

H.H. Austin was in the area in 1898 and reports that he found the country north of the Lake laid waste by the Ethiopians – all the cattle driven away, granaries burned to the ground and the crops in the fields destroyed. It appears that it was in this year that the Ethiopians made their first positive appearance in this corner of their Empire.

Welby, 1898

M.S. Welby, with a safari of Ethiopians, arrived at the Lake from Addis Ababa in the same year but owing to his unpopular followers, had little contact with the local tribes.

Donaldson-Smith, 1899

In 1899, Dr Donaldson-Smith made a second journey. He recorded that, during the four years which had elapsed since his previous visit, the formerly rich tribe of Rusia had ceased to exist, there being only a few groups of huts on the west bank of the Omo. Such was the result of Ethiopian penetration.

Maud, 1902-1903

In 1902-1903, Captain P. Maud reported that the Gelubba

were fearful and reserved. J.W. Brook, who was in this expedition, recorded that, when in the neighbourhood of Lake Rudolf, he encountered the advance guard of an Ethiopian force which had seized between thirty and forty thousand head of stock, as well as a great many slaves.

Gwynn, 1909

In 1909, Major C.W. Gwynn was in the area surveying the frontier. He wrote: 'reaching Lake Rudolf on February 22nd, we followed the shore northwards, passing an Abyssinian post on a slightly elevated spot just opposite the mouth of the Omo. In the neighbourhood of the post was a considerable settlement of Gelubba, a low-grade black tribe, allied to the Lokob[14] who cultivate and raise cattle for the Abyssinians'. Apparently, the remnants of the tribe, practically annihilated by the Ethiopians, were now collected together as their serfs.

Stigand, 1909

Also in 1909, C.H. Stigand ('To Abyssinia through an Unknown Land') visited the north end of the Lake and the first native he met said he was a 'Goliba'. It is Von Hohnel's opinion that, at the time of Count Teleki's expedition, the term 'Goliba' or 'Gheleba' was not applied to any one tribe and, in his opinion, it is the word meaning 'people in general' (cf. 'Bantu').

(3)
EVENTS ON THE GELUBBA BORDER 1913-1919
First recorded Gelubba raid, 1913

The first recorded Gelubba raid took place near Marsabit in May 1913, although it seems that in earlier years the Gelubba were frequently to be found mixed up in Ethiopian raiding parties. On this occasion, the raiders were attacked by a Somali constable and three armed camel-leaders who were looking after Government camels nearby; and as the raiders saw Rendille fighting men assembling in large numbers, they cleared off. The Rendille and Samburu recovered most of their stock and killed about twenty-five Gelubba, losing some fourteen men themselves. Ejerre Chudugleh[15] informed the writer in 1942 that the raiders had been guided to Marsabit by a renegade Rendille who was subsequently caught and stoned to death by the tribe.

First recorded action by the King's African Rifles against the Gelubba, 1913

In the same month, the Gelubba raided Samburu near Mount Kulal. They were engaged by a small party, under Captain J.H. Llewellyn, from the K.A.R. post at Loiyangolani and lost four killed and three wounded. About half the looted stock was recovered.

The 'Gabbra Massacres', 1913

At about this time, a series of raids and murders (generally referred to as the 'Gabbra Massacres') took place along the border, with the result that many refugees fled into Kenya territory. These raids were of course put down to the Gelubba ('Savages who had recently armed themselves with rifles and were out of control') by the Ethiopian authorities. It was, however, found later that, in at least one raid as far south as Maikona, some fifty Ethiopians were involved.[16]

Maikona Sub-Station, 1917

In 1917, Mr Harrington, Assistant District Commissioner Maikona, recorded that the Gelubba had taken to raiding on their own; presumably because up to this time they were usually mixed up with Ethiopians. Raids as far south as El Barta, Ndoto and Nyiro[17] and as far east as Maikona and Koronle are mentioned. The distinctive feature of Gelubba raids, even then, appears to have been the killing of people as opposed to preoccupation with loot; and Harrington thought this was the chief reason why their raids were so greatly feared by the Gabbra (during the 1941 raids, the Gelubba went so far as to slaughter stock they had no hope of getting away). Maikona was occupied as a sub-station for only a few months.

Occupation of Loiyangolani by the King's African Rifles, 1910-1917; recommendation to open Police post at North Horr, 1916

As early as 1916, it was recommended that a Police post be established at North Horr, in order to control the area from Lake Rudolf to the Hurri Hills; whilst from 1910 to 1917 there was a K.A.R. post at Loiyangolani. The former was originally intended to deal with Ethiopian ivory poachers and the latter with Turkana and Ethiopian raiders. No details are known of how these posts dealt with the Gelubba and their history has been lost in obscurity, no doubt a result of the constant changes from civil to military administration and vice versa which took place in the earlier decades of the century.

Maikona Police Post, 1917

Following the withdrawal of the Assistant District Commissioner from Maikona in 1917, a Constabulary post of about twelve men was sited there until it was taken over by the K.A.R. at the end of 1919. It is, however, recorded that in December 1918, the post had to be temporarily withdrawn 'through the professed inability of the Gabbra to supply either transport, meat or water for the police protecting them.' Gabbra cooperation in their own defense improved but little with the passing of years.

Raid on Rendille, 1919

In April 1919, the Gelubba raided the Rendille Urawein[18] near Kukum, killing fifty-seven people and capturing seven camels and a horse. The Rendille who have never taken kindly to being raided (unlike the Gabbra) followed up, aided by one constable and two Government camel leaders. Some forty Rendille were in the party and they succeeded in killing seventeen of the raiders and capturing seven rifles and bandoliers with ninety-nine rounds of Fusil Gras ammunition. Agen, then the Urawein headman, was killed in the raid.

(4)
THE FALL AND RISE OF THE GELUBBA, 1898-1918

When Europeans first came to know the Gelubba in 1888, they were a fairly powerful tribe, able to hold their own with other tribes; a part of the nicely balanced community of the peoples around the north of Lake Rudolf and along the Omo River. No better, but no worse than the others, they lived in a state of armed neutrality, open friendship or deadly enmity with their neighbours. Ten years later, the remnants of this once proud tribe had of necessity thrown in their lot with their conquerors; and by assisting them in raiding, they gradually amassed wealth and arms until they again became so powerful that they practically threw off the Ethiopian yoke and gained an ascendancy over the more numerous but less well-armed Turkana, Rendille and Samburu. These tribes maintained their integrity by pushing southwards with the advent of the Ethiopians in the delta area but lost the chance of obtaining arms in return for what sometimes proved to be inadequate protection from the Kenya Government. The Gabbra soon found themselves in a similar position.

(5)
THE MODERN GELUBBA 1940-1943

In 1940, the Gelubba were given additional arms by the Italians and proved themselves to be useful allies on many occasions. As the East African war moved northwards, military occupation of the northern Lake Rudolf area ceased. The Gelubba, now heavily armed, received further reinforcements in the way of army deserters from Italian units.

In 1942-1943, the Gelubba reached the zenith of their power. Raiding parties pushed far southwards on a scale unknown since the earlier years of the century; and for the first time in history, they staged planned attacks on police posts.

Rendille and Gabbra casualties were heavy. While the raiding parties suffered several reverses at the hands of the Kenya Police, the fact that the south-west corner of Ethiopia was unadministered made it all too easy for them to retreat to safety when the situation became too hot for them in Kenya territory.

As police reinforcements became available, the northern Kenya defence line was strengthened and Gelubba activities were confined to the border area. The Ethiopian authorities pushed their forces south-westwards to Lake Rudolf with the avowed intention of disarming the Gelubba and forcing them to pay compensation for the havoc wrought by their raiders during previous years. But it seemed certain that the Gelubba would continuously strain at any administrative bonds imposed on them.

SKETCH MAPS

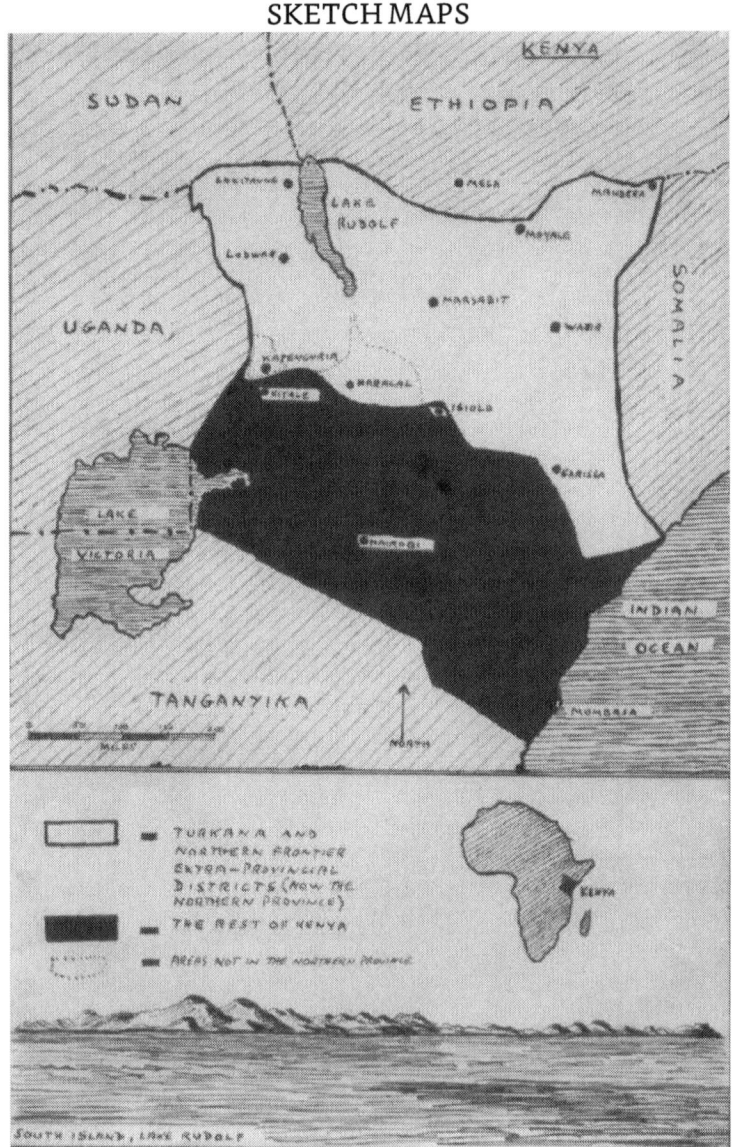

Figure 45: Sketch map of Kenya.

THE GLITTERING LAKE

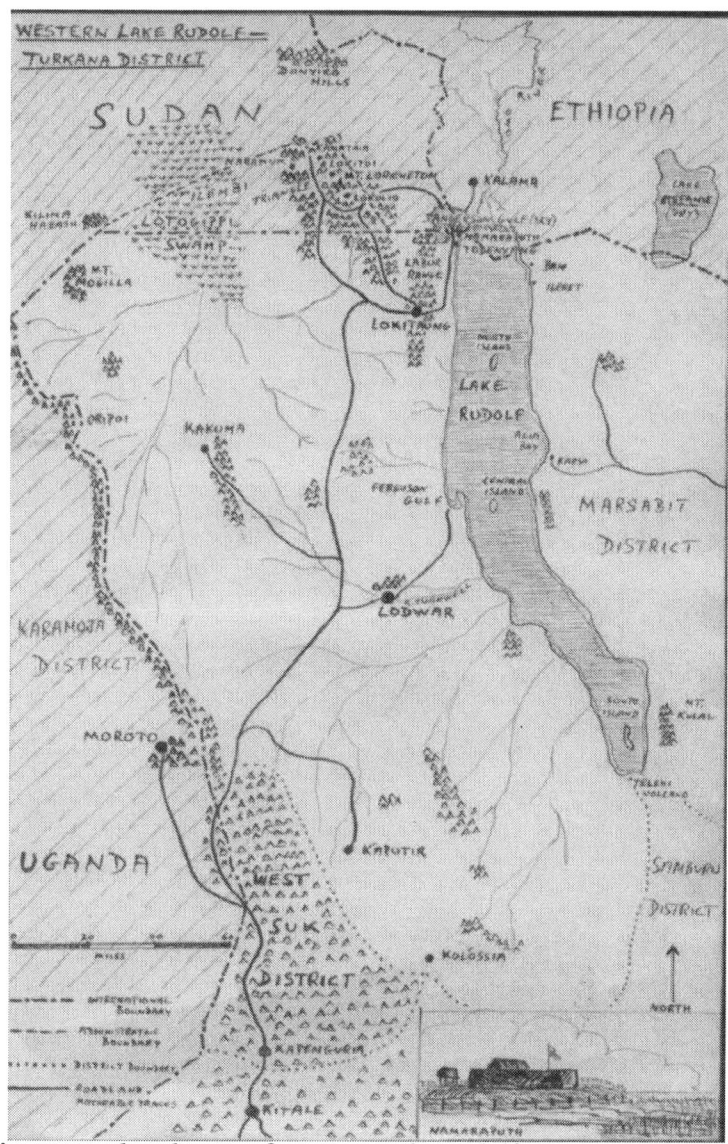

Figure 46: sketch map of western Lake Rudolf - Turkana District.

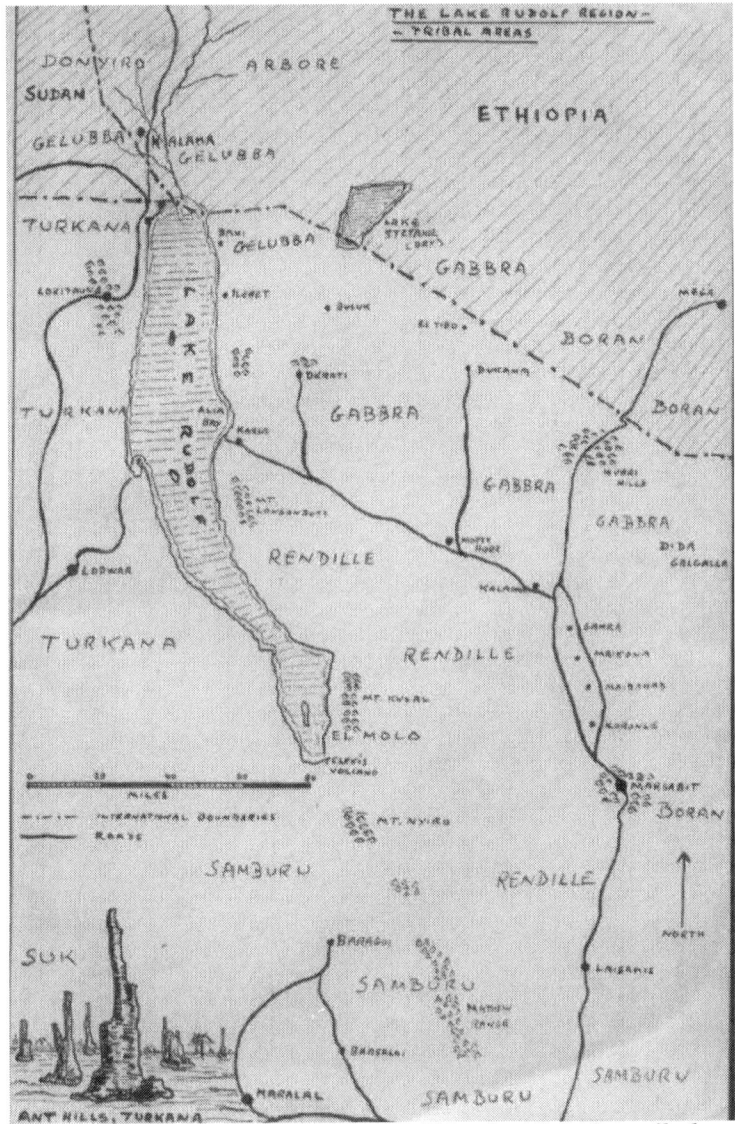
Figure 47: sketch map of the Lake Rudolf Region showing tribal areas.

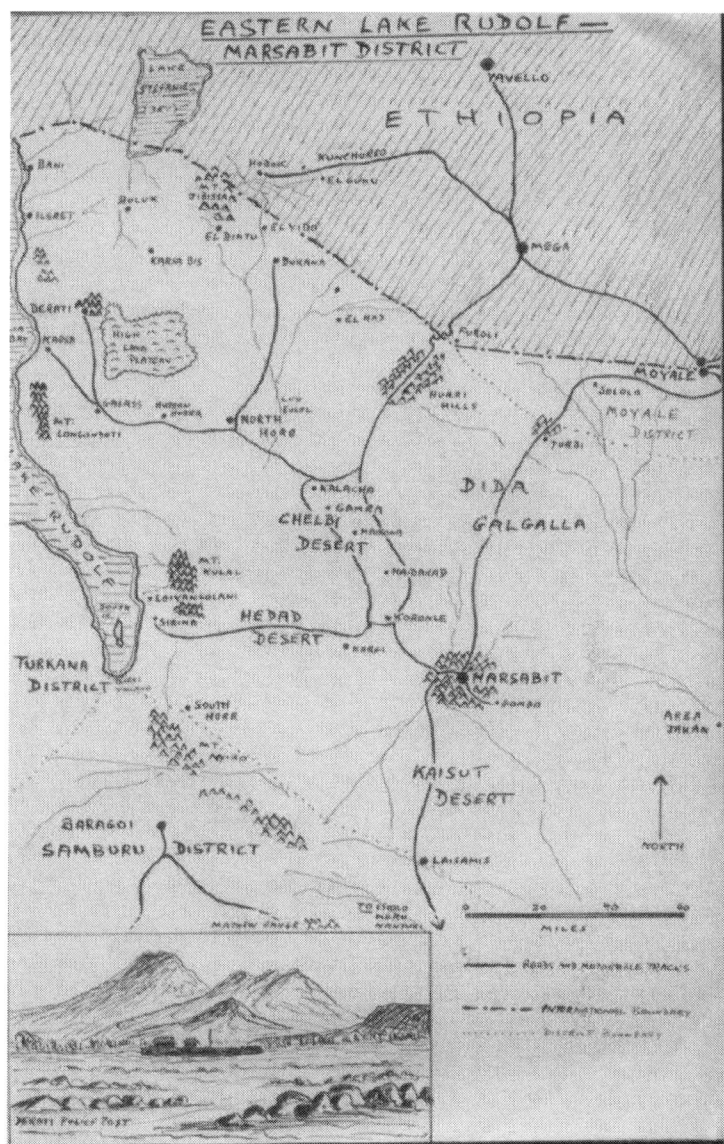

Figure 48: sketch map of Eastern Lake Rudolf - Marsabit District.

NOTES

1. The Geographical Journal, Vol. LXXXVI, No. 2, August 1935: The Lake Rudolph Rift-Valley Expedition 1934, by V.E Fuchs.
2. Irregular frontier troops.
3. Roughly equivalent to the rank of corporal.
4. Harold Hill died one morning in 1963 at the age of 82, sitting up in bed cracking open his boiled egg that was on the breakfast tray in front of him. He had still been working fulltime on his farm.
5. Donaldson-Smith: 'Through Unknown African Countries'.
6. The Elmolo by W.S.Dyson and V.E Fuchs: J. of the Royal Anthropological Institute, Vol. LXVII, July-December 1937.
7. The Geographical Journal Vol. LXXXVI, No. 2, August 1935 pp 118 and 133)
8. Now called Malawi.
9. From a paper read by Sir Vivian Fuchs on the Lake Rudolf Rift Valley Expedition 1934 to the Royal Geographical Society on 15 April 1935. (The Geographical Journal Vol. LXXXVI, No. 2, August 1935)
10. 'Discovery by Count Teleki of Lakes Rudolf and Stefanie' by Ludwig Von Hohnel. Pages 154-208, Vol. 2.
11. The facts related in the following extracts in this section were mostly taken direct from Admiral Ludwig von Hohnel's paper 'The Lake Rudolf Region: its discovery and subsequent exploration 1888-1909'. (Journal of the Royal African Society, January 1938).
12. A neighbouring tribe.
13. Turkana.
14. Samburu.
15. Rendille Government Headman.
16. Details of these events in 1913 may be found on pages

124 – 128 in the 'Jubaland and N.F.D. Handbook'.
17. All in the present Samburu country. El Barta is some 300 miles from the northern tip of Lake Rudolf.
18. A section of the Rendille tribe.

Printed in Germany
by Amazon Distribution
GmbH, Leipzig